Goulash and Picking Pickles

An almost boomer growing up
In rural Wisconsin
With recipes from Grandma and other relatives

Memoirs

By Louise Mae Hoffmann

Burning Daylight,
An imprint of Pearn and Associates, Inc.

Published by Burning Daylight
An imprint of Pearn & Associates, Inc., Fort Collins, Colorado
Contact us at 1600 Edora Ct. Ste. D, Fort Collins, CO 80525 (970) 599-8924.

Dustjacket cover design by Terence Orin (303) 444-0567

Conversion to paperback by Anne Kilgore.

Library of Congress Control Number: 2006904350

Hoffmann, Louise Mae,
Goulash and Picking Pickles / by Louise Mae Hoffmann. First Edition.

ISBN 978-0-9846523-5-8

Printed in the United States of America

For Gretchen, Marcus and David
Three very special children

TABLE OF CONTENTS

Chapters	Recipes
ACKNOWLEDGEMENTS / 6	
PROLOGUE / 8	
THE CYCLONE / 11	**Open jar pickles / 14**
AFTER THE STORM / 15	**Chocolate sauerkraut cake / 20**
THE CEMETERY / 21	**Vermont coffeecake / 24**
FRIENDSHIP / 25	**Mother's oatmeal cookies / 31**
JELLY FLUFF / 33	**Lasagna casserole / 38**
BICYCLING / 41	**Rhubarb cobbler / 46**
GRANDPARENTS / 47	**Grandma's nut bread / 56**
COUNTRY LIVING / 57	**Zucchini pickles / 62**
DOLLS / 63	**Heath bars / 65**
PAPER DOLLS / 67	**Five-minute fudge / 70**
THE SWING / 71	**Raised doughnuts / 74**
UP THE ROAD / 77	**Sweet pickles / 79**
CHURCH / 81	**Bundt chocolate cake / 88**
ONE ROOM SCHOOL / 89	**Copper pennies / 102**
LETTERS / 103	**Sliced pickles / 110**

TABLE OF CONTENTS continued

Acknowledgements:

I would like to thank my family and friends who through the years have shared their recipes with me. It is always fun to try new recipes, but the food that you've tasted at a friends house, or grew up with are always the best. I especially want to thank my sisters, LaVerne and LeAnne and sisters-in-law, Anita, Barbara, Marlene and Ruth for sharing their many recipes, particularly their numerous pickle recipes.

Also, I need to thank my friends and neighbors from all over the U.S. who through the years gave me recipes after sharing an especially good dinner: Arla, De, Donna, Helen, Irma, Jan, Judy, Rae, Susan, Mrs. Stahl and Mrs. Schwartz. Many of the recipes are from either my mother Mildred, Grandmother Louisa, or from my mother-in-law Bertha. I wish I had spent more time with them to learn more of their lives through their stories and recipes.

I want to thank several very good friends who have given me encouragement as I wrote these memoirs and shared with them bits and pieces of my life. Ginny, Anne, Irma, Grace and Lucy read the chapters and helped me edit and relate the writing from my point of view. A special note of thanks goes to my brothers-in-law, Otto and Willard who have been happy to share stories of farm and country life with me. Thank you also to Jeff who always believed I could write. Thanks also to Victor Pearn who had faith in my book when I was ready to give it up.

Also, I need particularly to thank my dear brother Loren and special friend Liv, who through the years have always been willing to listen and help me sort through parts of my life when it was hard for me to make sense of it all. And a special thank you to my children, Gretchen, Marcus and David who have always encouraged me and loved me no matter.

Also, I want to thank the many dear relatives, neighbors and friends from long ago who helped make my childhood. And while I have flown away, it is the place I have always seen as home and am glad that it played such a big part of my life. We learn of life through stories and the relatives, friends, and neighbors who make up our memories. This is how I remember growing up. Wisconsin will always be a part of me and I will take it with me no matter how far away I roam.

Louise Mae Hoffmann
May 4, 2006

PROLOGUE

CHILDHOOD…

Memories. What are memories? Is it that aspect of my life that shaped my future? Are memories necessary to live in the present? How far back do I need to go? Does my present shape my memories of the past?

So little of one's life is spent there, yet the memories linger on, longer than any other period of life. My quick impressions are country, rural Wisconsin, farmland, German traditions, hard work, be tough. God was harsh. Easy life was a sinful life.

Memories. I look back.

I remember dancing in the driveway acting out "My Fair Lady" and singing at the top of my lungs, pretending I was on the Broadway stage.

I remember playing in the leaves in our front yard, building an outline of a house, complete with rooms and furnishings. I remember also the outhouse and growing hollyhocks in front of it to disguise it.

I remember walking home with Richard each day after school. We walked slowly as he had asthma. He would have to stop, stoop, and catch his breath before he could go on.

I remember vividly the cyclone with the thundering, lightning, and trees crashing down. I continued praying to God night after night for many years that we would never have such a storm again, and thanking Him for saving my little brother Loren.

I remember riding my bike all around the countryside, pedaling against the wind and feeling its force in my face.

I remember my dad, teaching and preaching. I believe he never really let go of his job, its headaches and concerns. I realize now how his call into the teaching ministry permeated our whole life as a family.

I remember my mother trying to make "ends meet" and never quite succeeded, asking over and over again, "Why couldn't my dad earn more money?"

I always wondered why my parents couldn't get along. Why did they always argue and never seem to agree on anything? They were each nice people in their own way, but together they exploded like dynamite.

I remember my childhood as pleasant, happy, sad and at times explosive. Can I look back as an observer and see it more clearly as an adult? What aspects of it did I pass on to my children?

Louise Mae Hoffmann

THE CYCLONE

"Please God; don't let any more trees fall down on our yard. And thank you God for not letting any trees fall on our house and thank you God for keeping Loren safe."

Night after night I recited the litany of those three prayers for over fifteen years. I became worried that if I didn't say those prayers maybe God would forget and another storm would come and send trees down on our house. What a worry to a child!

The terrible storm, called a cyclone, was the summer I turned five. It was a terrifying summer storm. **BOOM! CRASH! BANG! FLASH!** Thunder, lightning. Then there was a pause. Then more thunder and more lightning. The trees were blowing and bending over.

The World Book Dictionary defines a cyclone as (1) "A storm or winds moving around and spiraling in toward a calm center of low pressure, which also moves. The winds of a cyclone move counterclockwise in the Northern Hemisphere and clockwise in the Southern Hemisphere. (2) Any very violent windstorm, such as a tornado."

In the summer months Wisconsin has many cyclones and tornadoes. This was the one I remember. My new baby brother was asleep in the back room. How did he sleep through all the noise? I don't know. It was early evening. The sky was black, except when the flashes of lightning lit up the whole countryside. And then the big crack came. **Ka-boom! Ka-boom! Ka-boom!** What was that? Dare we look? We went out onto the front porch. It was still raining buckets. Crack, another, and then another and another peal of thunder. And within seconds the lightning followed the thunder.

How did the lightning miss the house?

And then almost as quickly as the storm started, it was over. And oh my, what a sight to behold. Four big trees on the front lawn and one tree in the back yard all lay on their side. Their roots were lying exposed. Five huge, magnificent trees came down on our yard, all within inches of our house. But not one tree touched our house.

Some of my friends had a cyclone cellar where they stayed during the storm. My house had a fruit cellar, but my parents didn't think it was necessary to go down it during the storm. We were told that God would keep us safe.

I grew up with this dichotomy of how God worked. God loved you and protected you. He watched over you. But if you were bad, you would be punished. God expects you to be good and obey your parents. God loves you; He is all-powerful, so if you are not good you will be punished.

I was told Jesus loved me, and He died for all my sins. But I should be good and not sin.

I was scared of God, but at the same time knew I needed Him to protect me. I wanted to be good. I didn't always know what was expected of me though.

I wanted to do all I could so that God would love and protect me.

The night of the Cyclone my prayers began: "Thank you God for keeping our house safe, please God don't send another storm to knock down any more trees, and thank you God for keeping Loren safe, in Jesus' name. Amen."

The house is safe to this day.

OPEN JAR PICKLES

1 gallon water
1 cup vinegar
1 cup salt
1 teaspoon alum

Boil the above ingredients.
Let cool.
Pour over pickles.
Cover with cotton cloth
Let sit 2 weeks and eat from open jar.

Summer treat.

AFTER THE STORM

The neighbors across the road also had trees fall down on their yard. In a few days they were having a wedding. It was a very special wedding for I was to be the flower girl. Oh, what fun and excitement!

The farmers came with their big tractors to help haul away the huge tree trunks. Leaves, branches and dirt were everywhere. Big saws were set up with the tractors to cut through the huge maple tree trunks. It was very loud. The machines were all making a tremendous racket, chop, crunch, chop and crunch was heard throughout the neighborhood. Everyone helped the neighbors, as the wedding was only two days away. It was fascinating to watch the men work, although the men didn't let us children to stand too close to the big tractor.

It was hard work to pull the massive tree trunk out of the hole. It was over fifteen feet in diameter.

First, the men cut the big branches of the tree away from the trunk and hauled these to a field in back of the barn. After all the big branches were hauled away, the remaining trunk and roots were attached with a huge chain to the big tractor. The tractor pulled and pulled.

Finally it came out of its big hole. The roots were chopped up by another machine. They were then used to fill the hole back up. Finally the big job was over.

The men then had to go to our house as my parent's house really belonged to the congregation. The men of the congregation had to take care of all the extraordinary repairs. Four trees had come down on our front lawn. It was a big job. The trees all had to be cut into logs and the roots pulled out and hauled away. The men had a big job to do after this big storm.

Inside the house, other wedding preparations were being done. The reception was at the home of the bride. Everything had to be cleaned and polished. The bride's mother and her friends were busy preparing fruit pies, chocolate and white cakes. Ham and egg salad sandwiches all had to be made as neighbors and relatives from near and far were coming. This was before the day of big home freezers so most of the food preparation had to be done the last few days before the wedding to insure freshness.

My mother was sewing me a very special flower girl dress. My mother had purchased white taffeta fabric. It matched the bride's dress except it didn't have a long train. It reached the floor and had an extra fancy ruffle at the bottom. I had new white sandals to wear.

I was to stand up next to Evelyn in church. Evelyn, the bride-to-be, had always been very special to me. I went over often to visit her and she would let me look at her make-up, jewelry, and her fancy clothes. She was much more grown up than my sisters who were still in high school. Sometimes she would give me a bracelet I could keep, or an old pair of high-heeled shoes to play with. Then I would go home and pretend I was grown-up and going to work or getting married.

We had a rehearsal for the wedding the Friday night before the wedding. I was told that I had to stand very still. I was NOT to move. I was known as a "wiggle-worm" and a talker, especially in church. This always got me into trouble. Spankings didn't seem to cure me. It seemed impossible to sit still through the long church service on those hard wooden pews. It wasn't fair. It wasn't that I didn't like church; I just didn't like to sit still. Did God really mind?

I was told very severely by my mother that I was not to wiggle standing up front in church. I knew that my Dad would be up on the organ bench. Even with his back toward the altar he could still see me in his mirror which was above the organ. He would probably jump off his organ bench, run down the balcony steps, hurry down the aisle and spank me in front of the bride. Horrors! I must stand still.

And still I did stand. I wouldn't even twitch for a fly that landed on my nose. I didn't smile either for I was so scared. I'm not sure if I was more afraid of God or my father.

The wedding pictures show a scared little girl in a pretty long taffeta dress standing near the bride, as stiff as a board. My hair was curled tight. My mother had given me a home permanent wave just the week before. But I received no spankings on Evelyn's wedding day.

After the church services I began to relax a little. But who were all these men at the wedding? What did they have to do with the bride? Nobody told me about men at the wedding! The groom maybe should be there, but all these other men, who needed them? In the pictures taken by the special wedding photographers I look like a scared little girl.

The dinner was at the hotel in our neighboring town. I had never even eaten at a restaurant, so this was another strange new experience. And I had to sit with all these strangers. The bride was too busy to pay much attention to me. I had been told to behave. And that meant no wiggling and no talking. Weddings sure weren't much fun. There were all kinds of different food. Glasses, lots of silverware, small plates and big plates. What was I to do? I must have been ready to cry, for the bride decided that maybe I should sit next to my parents who were in the next room. Maybe I would smile then. I think my parents were a bit ashamed of me, as I really didn't know how to behave. No one thought of telling a little girl in those days what to expect. I was just supposed to know.

I was to sit and watch. I was supposed to figure things out on my own. I was not to ask questions. I was to be seen and not heard. Oh my, I felt I had goofed again.

Somehow I got through the meal and everybody went to the bride's house.

This was better! The men took off their suit jackets, the music jamboree started, and all the special food was set out. The beer barrel was opened. I was given soda pop to drink. I could have as much as I wanted. High school students were allowed to drink beer. This was common at most family celebrations at home. There was lots of laughter and jokes. All the guests were having a good time.

It was time to open the wedding gifts. The flower girl got to hold the ribbons. My friends from the neighborhood were there and I could show off my dress, my new shoes, and my flowers. I could twirl my dress to the music. My picture got taken. Being a flower girl was fun after all. The memories of standing still and being scared would only show up afterwards in the pictures.

CHOCOLATE SAUERKRAUT CAKE

1/2 cup margarine (butter)
1 teaspoon baking soda
1 1/2 cups sugar
1/4 teaspoon salt
3 eggs
1/2 cup cocoa
1 teaspoon vanilla
1 cup water
2 cups sifted flour
1 cup sauerkraut, drained, rinsed, and chopped
1 teaspoon baking powder

Cream margarine and sugar until light and fluffy
Beat in eggs, one at a time
Add vanilla.
Sift together flour, baking powder, soda, salt and cocoa;
Add to creamed mixture alternately with water, beating after each addition.
Stir in sauerkraut.
Turn into greased and floured 13” x 9” baking pan.
Bake at 350 degrees for 35 to 40 minutes.
Cool in pan.

FROSTING
Melt one 6-ounce pkg. semisweet chocolate pieces and
4 tablespoons margarine over low heat.
Remove from heat
Blend in 1/2 cup sour cream, 1 teaspoon vanilla and 1/4 teaspoon salt.
Gradually add sifted confectioners' sugar (2 1/2 to 3 cups) to make spreading consistency; Beat well.
Frost on cooled cake… Enjoy!

THE CEMETERY

Between the country church and the school was the cemetery. It was fun to walk around the different tombstones. Some were big. Some were very small. They came in all colors: red, gray, and white were the most common colors. There were some new ones at the front near the church, with the real old ones nearer the school building. Some headstones had fallen down and sometimes I remember trying to prop them up. Some had strange names on them, but most of the names were familiar names just like the people in church: Klemp, Schroeder, Hoewish and Tews.

This is where people went when they died. That is, when Jesus wanted them. This was only their bones. The dead people got a new body from Jesus and were up in heaven with Him, somewhere high up in the sky. This was before man walked on the moon, so anywhere further than an airplane could fly was probably close to heaven.

Heaven was a big fancy house that God took care of. No more dirty dishes or scrubbing floors. God had this beautiful castle in the sky.

The cemetery was a place of deep fascination to me, a little girl of five. I wasn't quite sure how God got you there, but somehow once you got buried, Jesus carried you off to heaven to be with God.

And then one day, Rev. Tornow died. He was my friend. He didn't seem to mind my wiggling in church, only my Dad did. And he lived with Mrs. Tornow, my special friend. She would let me sit next to her in church sometimes. That was special. It was kind of like sitting next to my Grandma. But of course I didn't see my Grandma much as she lived too far away. On Sundays we had to go to our church, because my Dad had to play the organ.

But now, Rev. Tornow was dead. I don't remember how he died, but I do remember seeing him in the coffin, all stiff, with a slight smile on his lips. And then they closed the lid. I think some hymns were sung, and the Bible was read. I don't remember wiggling in church. I was too fascinated by the coffin.

What was going to happen next? Then the coffin was carried out of the church by some of the men and out to the cemetery. A big hole had been dug. Ropes were around the hole, and the coffin was carefully placed on the ropes. The men let the ropes go and the coffin got lowered down into the hold. They were burying the minister. This is what they did to dead people. I hadn't been sure. How God got the person after this, no one ever explained to me. Maybe grown-ups didn't know either. Maybe it happened at night when everyone was asleep. Maybe you became invisible and floated up past the clouds. But now, at least I knew how one got in the ground.

Some more words were spoken. Dirt was thrown on the coffin. It seemed a shame to cover up such a pretty box. Shovelful by shovelful the coffin got buried, and then flowers got put on the top of the dirt. People left.

Food was prepared by the church ladies in the church basement. It seemed almost like a church picnic. Everyone was visiting and talking. But Rev. Tornow wasn't there, and Mrs. Tornow seemed so sad.

Before many weeks past, she moved away. The house didn't seem the same. It took a long while to get a new minister. I didn't know why. It was such a nice house. But times maybe were changing and winters were long and the country living was not the same for an adult as it was for a child.

But Rev. Tornow stayed. A special big white cross got put over the place where he was buried. It's still there and I still see the smile on his face.

VERMONT COFFEECAKE

1 stick margarine
2 cups flour
1 cup sugar
1 cup plain yogurt or sour cream
1 teaspoon almond extract
1 teaspoon baking soda
1 teaspoon baking powder
2 eggs
Pinch of salt

Cream margarine and sugar
Blend in eggs and yogurt
Add almond extract
Set aside
Sift together dry ingredients
Gently mix wet and dry ingredients together
Batter can be lumpy
Take batter and twice alternate it with the Topping which follows:

TOPPING

1 teaspoon cinnamon
½ cup brown sugar
½ cup nuts
Sprinkle top with raisins or chocolate chips
Bake 350 for 35 minutes
Invert and cool in pan.

Simply delicious.

FRIENDSHIP

The happiest times that I remember as a child are those when I was playing in my sandbox with my friend Richard. It allowed us to escape into a world of fantasy. It was a world we created and set the rules.

Richard and I often played all day in the sandbox. He lived next door on the farm. Richard had asthma. He couldn't run around or help out with the farm chores as many of the neighborhood children did. He liked to play in the sandbox with me.

My sandbox was our old tin bathtub. It was ideal. It had high sides of twenty inches and was about five feet long and two feet across. My dad got the sand for me from the sand pit. This was a big hill on the side of the road about five miles from our house. He would fill up several big old gunny sack bags of sand for me to play in. It was lovely red sand, very smooth, and when wet it would pack extremely well.

We loved to make ice cream cones using a small metal cup from an old doll dish set. We would fill the cup up with sand and pack it very tightly. Then we would tip it out by hitting it gently on the bottom. Presto. It looked just like a scoop of ice cream.

We would stack the scoops higher and higher until they would topple over. Sometimes Richard and I would try to eat them, but usually we just pretended to eat them as the sand didn't taste very good.

Richard didn't have a sandbox like I did, but at his house we could play in the dirt under his porch. That was almost as good. We sometimes played with the toy trucks, hauling dirt back and forth to make roads and villages. We would take turns playing at his house and then at my house. We never got into fights.

One day we decided to wash all the toys in the sandbox. We found a couple of old buckets. They were heavy to lift even without water in them. We carried the buckets over to the faucet by the house. We filled them up to the top.

My mother suggested we carry the sand box toys to the bucket. We thought we could carry the bucket down to the sandbox. I didn't like to be told what to do. I thought I could carry the bucket by myself.

I lifted up the big black bucket, and oops, right down on my toe it dropped. Ouch, did it hurt! I was so mad at myself that I didn't cry. I didn't like to be told that I couldn't do something. I didn't like it that my mother was right. It seems I had so many lessons to learn.

Before long, my big toe nail turned black and blue. And then it started getting loose. I was going to lose my toe nail.

My mother told me that I would be getting a new toe nail. It would grow back before I was married.

Richard and I sometimes played in the leaves in the fall. We loved to make leaf houses. We usually did this on my front yard. We had only box elder trees on my front yard and we didn't have enough leaves for a leaf house. Mrs. Klemp, the neighbor across the street, had big oak and maple trees. She was my friend. I was the flower girl at her daughter's wedding the summer I was five.

We went over to the Klemp's house and asked Mrs. Klemp if we could have some of their leaves. She was very happy to let us have some of their leaves.

Richard and I got our wagons. We filled them up with leaves. We went back and forth across the road. We got many wagon loads of leaves.

Finally we thought we had enough leaves to make a leaf house. We outlined a big house with leaves. We put in many rooms and doorways. We even made furniture for our house out of the leaves. We made beds, davenports, and chairs. We had a very big fancy house.

We played "house" until it got dark outside. We pretended we were the mother and the father. Our pets also were in the house.

In the fall it got dark early, but those few special weeks before winter set in were special times.

Sometimes, Richard and I would pack a small picnic lunch and head up to the big woods. First we would go past the little woods, and then the upper garden, and then we would come to the big woods. We would follow the trail and find the trash dump.

In the country families did not get their trash picked up by big trash trucks. Everybody had to find their own place for their trash. My dad burned as much of our trash as he could in the furnace or out on a pile in the field next to the garden.

Peelings and roots would get thrown out to the garden. In the spring they would be turned into the dirt. But the cans and glass that didn't burn got put in the big aluminum can in back of our garage. This can had a hook on it that my dad could attach to the back of the car. When it got full he would attach the big can to the car and drive it up to the big woods. There he dumped it onto the very big pile of trash from many years.

It was always fun to see what made it up to the woods. There was always an assortment of tin cans and broken bottles, but sometimes we found a piece of broken furniture.

Other people from the church were allowed to haul their junk up there also if they didn't have a place of their own. Maybe we would find a broken cage that we could crawl in and out of. Sometimes we found a pretty bottle that someone threw out. After we checked out the whole junk pile, Richard and I would continue into the woods. We would follow the trail and looked for the pretty violets and other wild flowers. We also had to watch out for "cow pies." Cows are big animals and leave a distinctive very big round pile of excrement.

There was a fence separating the woods from the farmer's fields on each side of the woods. But sometimes the cows broke through the fence and enjoyed eating the fresh grass in the woods.

We were not afraid of the cows. They were fun to watch. The farmers usually kept their bull in the barnyard near the barn. The bull was the only animal that you had to be careful of. Sometimes they could get mean.

The cows though were gentle and would let us rub their noses. They were velvety soft. It wasn't fun though to step in a "cow pie." It would mess up your shoes and you would smell the odor the rest of the day.

Richard and I would find a nice grassy spot and have our picnic lunch. We often had home made coffeecake, some Kool-

Aid, an apple and maybe a carrot. We would have all our favorite foods. We didn't take anything we didn't like to eat like beets or spinach. Those foods we had to eat at dinner time.

Sometimes I ate dinner at Richard's house. His dad seemed even stricter than my dad. He would put the portion of food on your plate that he expected you to eat. I had to eat all my beets on my plate before he would let me get up to play. I was afraid of him. I liked Richard's mom. She was young and had a little girl and boy besides Richard. I think she was afraid of the father also.

In late summer Richard's mother and his two aunts would make soap. They would do this after his dad and uncles had butchered the pigs for their winter meat. There would be big tubs of lard that they would heat over an outdoor fire. Then Richard's aunts stirred and stirred. It was very hot. We weren't allowed to get very close.

After a couple of days the soap would be ready. It was big hard chunks. It wasn't very pretty. It was usually a light brown. They would break the chunks into smaller pieces and give some to my mother. She would use this soap for washing clothes. I never could understand how lard turned into soap, but I know it did.

Another thing that Richard's aunts did was make sausage. The meat would have to be ground up. Then it was stirred over the fire. It was put in a casing which came from the dead pig. Then it was put into the smokehouse where it would hang up on a piece of gut string. There was a smoky fire by the smokehouse. It usually smelled good. I knew before long there would be some good summer sausage to eat.

Richard and I stayed pals all through grade school. We often walked home from school together.

Richard often had to stop and bend over to help him breathe. It was hard for me to see him suffer. He never complained though. He was a good friend.

In high school his family moved to the city as his asthma was getting worse. They needed to get Richard away from the hay and the cows.

I saw him a few times after that as his cousins still lived in the country and he would come with his family to visit them. After high school I heard that he got married and had two children.

But one day he got the flu. He was getting better, but then he had a coughing spell. He choked and died. I was so sad. Richard's aunts told my mother about it.

He was a good friend. We never got mad at each other. We were just good friends. I know someday I will be with him again in heaven and we will share the memories of our childhood friendship.

MOTHER'S OATMEAL COOKIES

3/4 cup vegetable shortening
1 cup firmly packed brown sugar
1/2 cup granulated sugar
1 egg
1/4 cup water
1 teaspoon vanilla
3 cups uncooked oatmeal
1 cup flour
2 teaspoon baking soda
Nuts, raisins or coconut can be added

Cream shortening with sugars
Add egg, water and vanilla
Add baking soda
Stir in oatmeal and flour
Make into round balls and flatten gently with fork
Bake at 375 degrees for 10 - 12 minutes.

Hide some away or they'll be gone in a day.

JELLY FLUFF

Pets were very much a part of my growing up. As far back as I can remember as a child my family had cats, kittens, a dog of some mixed breed and for quite a few years Angora rabbits.

Generally the cats belonged to me. Sally was the mother to Jelly Fluff and Jam. How Sally, a dark striped tiger cat bore Fluffy, a gray fluffy Angora cat and Jam, a skinnier short-haired version I never learned.

They were the best kittens. I treated them like my doll babies. Jelly and Jam were brother and sister. I gave them my doll's baby bottles. They promptly clawed and chewed the nipples into small pieces.

When they were kittens I dressed them up in my doll's clothes. They didn't really like it, but I thought they looked so cute. They particularly objected to the bonnet! Getting the bonnet tied under their chin took all of my patience and by the time I was done my hand was all scratched up.

I remember looking at my hands and arms, wondering if this is how they were suppose to look, red, scratchy and full of scabs! My mother always said my hands would be healed by the time I got married!

Once I got the dolls dressed I would give them a buggy ride. At this time my little brother was getting too big for the buggy or baby carriage, the more formal name. I guess my mother figured she wouldn't need it for any more children. Five seemed enough mouths to feed. She let me use the buggy to play with to my heart's content.

Sometimes I would push my brother in it just for fun. We didn't have a real long sidewalk, about twenty feet. It was the smoothest piece of concrete around. The black buggy had been purchased for the older children, when my parents lived in the city. They moved to the country eighteen days after I was born. I wondered if I ever received buggy rides.

Those first winters in the country we didn't even have indoor plumbing or running water. It would seem my mother would not have had time to push me in any carriage. And where would she have pushed me? The sidewalk was put in after they remodeled the house and I was already five years old.

After my brother was born, my sisters would sometimes give me a ride with him in the buggy. Sometimes my mother yelled at them for going as fast as she was afraid they would lose balance and we might tip over.

Pushing the cats in the buggy was a real problem. The problem was keeping the cats inside the buggy. They were always trying to climb out.

My cats also got baptized. I figured if baptism was so important for babies and dolls, it certainly was important for kittens. Putting the water on their head was the tricky part.

Sally had a sister named Susie. Susie was OK, but her main gift was to keep giving us a new supply of kittens. Once she had a litter of five that I got to name. Since I already had Jelly and Jam, I decide to go with berry names: Strawberry, Blueberry, Raspberry, and Blackberry. And then, wow, I had a great idea. Being almost the baby of the family, but couldn't behave like one because I had a baby brother, I was often told to be quiet. Often my sisters would yell, "Shut-up Louise." Well, I would show them. I decided to name the fifth kitten, Shut Up. Then when I was asked my kitten's name I could say Shut Up, and I'd be telling the truth. I didn't think I could get punished for that!

I am sad to say, Shut Up was the puniest of the five kittens and died before I really got full value out of her name!

The other kittens were all given away as my mother thought two cats were enough. Sally and Susie were given to my cousin's on their farm seventy miles away.

What a surprise! Several weeks later Sally returned to our house. She found her way back without a road map, through the fields of the Wisconsin countryside. This time, my mother allowed her to stay, but I don't remember her having any more kittens. Maybe the long walk back took out any desire she had to travel off our property. Or perhaps she knew my mother wouldn't tolerate any more kittens!

Fluffy lived to a ripe old age and was even allowed in the living room, a rare privilege. Growing up on the farm, my mother generally held with the premise that pets, although nice, belonged outside. At Christmas time, Fluffy even got bows in his fur and had his picture taken under the Christmas tree.

Fluffy was always around. He caught a few mice now and then. He ate outside though and was fed leftover scraps. My family never even considered buying pet food in a store. It was costly enough buying food for the five children. On cold winter days, my mother would let Fluffy eat down in the basement.

Fluffy understood me. I could sit and talk to him for hours and he'd listen. Sometimes, just being around me as I was doing my chores, or staying close by after I received a scolding was all the comfort I would need. Fluffy accepted me as I was. He never expected more than I could give. What more could a person ask of a friend?

Fluffy died shortly after I went off to college.

We had a number of dogs when I was young. Spotty was the favorite. He was a really gentle, sweet dog. He got run over by a car. I remember how sad we all were, and my mother thought we shouldn't get any more pets. But we did.

Tippy was a really feisty black dog. One day when he was outside tied on his chain, it got all wrapped up around my little brother. I saw him standing there as I was playing outside. I screamed, "Mommy." It gave us a real scare. What if I hadn't seen it and called my mom for help? Usually our dogs weren't tied up, but Tippy was always running out on the road. After the incident with my brother, Tippy was sent away to a farm family where he could run free.

My older brother had the idea to raise angora rabbits for earning money. He would breed them, and clip their fur and then sent the fur off to a company. At one time, he had over a dozen rabbits. Again, I got to name them. I also got to feed them. My brother built the pens, but then was busy with his other jobs and so hired me to feed and water them.

This was an easy job to do in the summer, fall and spring. But in the winter it was a quite unpleasant task. The water dishes were old tin cans. I would punch a hole in them and with wire fasten them to the side of the rabbits pen. Even then, the rabbits could often tip over the can of water. But worse than that in the winter, the water always froze. So, each day I would have to try to unfasten the frozen water tin and tie on a fresh tin with water. I would do this twice a day. The rabbits also got pellets to eat.

In the summer I could pull fresh grass, and other garden greens for them, but in the winter the main food they had were pellets. My brother paid me ten cents a week for my endeavor.

My mother got the job of clipping the rabbits. I would help her by holding down the legs.

Clipping a wiggly rabbit was not an easy task. She had to do this on the kitchen table. It would be done in the late spring, after the freezing weather was over. It takes a lot of rabbit fur to make a pound. I don't think this was one of my brother's most successful investments! But, it was fun.

LASAGNA CASSEROLE

1 pound ground beef
1 tablespoon parsley flakes
1 clover garlic, minced (or garlic flakes)
1 tablespoon basil
1 1/2 teaspoon salt
1, 16oz. can tomatoes (2 cups)
1, 6 oz. cans tomato paste
I often double the sauce, and use one can tomato paste and one can tomato sauce.
10 oz. lasagna or wide noodles, cooked ahead of time

1 cup cream style cottage cheese
2 beaten eggs
2 teaspoon salt
½ teaspoon pepper
2 tablespoon parsley flakes
½ cup grated Parmesan cheese
1 pound mozzarella cheese or other favorite cheese sliced thin

Brown meat slowly, spooning off excess fat
Add next 6 ingredients
Simmer uncovered until sauce is thick, 45 minutes to 1 hour, stirring occasionally.
Cook noodles in boiling salted water until tender; drain, rinse in cold water.

Meanwhile combine cottage cheese with eggs,
seasonings and Parmesan cheese.
Place half of the cooked noodles in 13x9x2 baking dish.
Spread half of the cottage cheese mixture over the
lasagna noodles.
Add half of the mozzarella cheese and half of the
meat sauce.
Repeat layers.
Bake in 375 oven for 30 minutes.
Let stand 15 minutes before cutting into squares.
Makes 12 servings.

Serve with green garden salad and fresh baked bread.

Wonderful for company dinner as can be prepared ahead of time.

BICYCLING

Learning to ride a big bike was the first big step I had as a child to become an independent traveler. A tricycle was okay when I was a toddler, but when I was getting ready to start school, I yearned to ride a bike, a two-wheeler.

There were bikes in the garage. My big brother Lyle hardly ever rode his bike as he was in high school already and was allowed to drive the family car. But his bike was too hard for a five-year-old to even consider mounting. My two older sisters didn't want me riding their bicycles for fear I would get them all scratched up. What was I to do?

My Dad was always out visiting various church members, especially those with children in the home. One day on his rounds he stopped at the Otto's. They had twin girls my brother's age. They didn't need their bikes anymore. They would be happy to sell my dad one of their bikes for me. The bicycle was almost new. It was wonderful. It was green. The bike was very heavy. This was in the days before skinny wheels and hand brakes. It felt like it weighed fifty pounds. It had a front basket fastened in front of the handle bars, and a rear bumper on it so that I could attach saddlebags.

Saddlebags were wonderful. Maybe I would get some for my birthday. I saw a pair of black ones when I was in town the last time with my dad. I could store all sorts of things in a pair of saddlebags. Books, food, and my school jacket were just a few of the things I could put in the saddlebags. The bike was very heavy. I could hardly hold it up.

How was I ever going to learn to ride it? The bicycle felt so enormous. It seemed so heavy. I didn't think that I would ever be able to balance myself. I became very frustrated and angry at myself.

My good friend Janice knew how to ride already, so I wanted to learn as quickly as possible. I tried and tried. I fell many times. I scraped my knees. I cried. I thought I would never learn how to ride my new bicycle.

Then one afternoon my big brother walked and walked alongside the bike holding it steady for me. He let go after a while and I found myself going all by myself. What a glorious feeling. It was wonderful.

I rode all over our yard. I went faster and faster. When I rode on the bumpy, stony driveway I went bump, bump. I didn't care. Soon I was trying it out with one hand and then no hands. What an exhilarating feeling. It was marvelous!

I started to beg my mother to let me ride the bike out on the road. "Please, please," I cried, "I'll be very careful."

My mother finally said, "Yes, you may go out on the road, but be very careful to look for cars."

I was off. I was exploring a new world.

My bicycle opened another new world for me to explore. No longer would I be limited to visiting the neighbors between my house and the church. Now I could ride to Judy's house, or to Janice's house, or stop at Rogene's along the way. And not too much further past Judy's house was Joyce's. A whole new world opened to me.

"Please, Mom, let me go. I'll be home by 3 o'clock,"

"Be very, very careful!"

"O.K., bye."

Our road was still gravel, so travel by bicycle was tricky. It was worn down gravel, so if I went on the worn tire tracks, it was usually navigable.

Then one day in late spring I discovered that the road was going to be blacktopped. That would be glorious. With a smooth road I would really be able to fly on my bike.

Before blacktop was poured, the roadbed had to be prepared. Truck loads of new gravel were poured on the road in preparation.

It was the day before the school spring program. Everyone was excited. It was the big school event of the year. School was about over. Studies were ready to be set aside.

A stage had been built in the church basement. A stage curtain was hung and could be drawn open and closed. Poems and other recitations have been given out. Several one-act plays would be performed. It was the day before the final dress rehearsal.

It was time to leave for school. By now, I felt I'd mastered my bike. I was finishing first grade. My bike had lost its rubber pedal. I had to be extra careful about my shoe sliding off the metal round bar that usually held the rubber pedal. I peeled out of the driveway as it was almost time for the school bell to ring. It would take about five minutes to pedal my bicycle to school. My sister was way ahead of me, walking her bicycle and talking to some friends.

Oops, the new big rough gravel stones were worse than I expected. As I rounded the corner of my driveway and attempted to gather speed my shoe slipped off the metal bar, and down I went! My bare knees go down on the gravel. The big bike fell on top of me.

I shouted, "LeAnne, Help! Help!" She ignored my cry. The excuse that she gave our mother afterward was that she was almost at the schoolhouse when she heard me. It was too far back to turn around and come back to help me. And she added, "Besides, Louise is always crying and shouting at her when she was ahead getting to school."

I was ruined. My knee hurt and my dress was all bloody. "What will Mama say, I wonder?" I limped back to the house. My knee was still bleeding. Blood was everywhere. What a mess I'm in. I'd be late to school for sure. Mama came out as she hears my wailing.

"Oh, poor Louise," my mother said. In a minute she saw it was no ordinary scratch. The bike bar jabbed into my knee. I would need more than a Band-Aid. Mama led me to our porch steps. She rushed in the house for a wet rag. Have I broken my leg, she wondered?

I'd hurt my pride more than anything. I thought I could handle the rough gravel stones. Mama ran over to the neighbors for help. I needed to go to the doctor. Mama didn't drive a car. The neighbor man offered to drive us to the doctor's. His wife would watch my little brother.

I was very upset. I didn't like going to the doctor. I didn't want him to touch me. I knew I must go because my knee hurt a whole lot.

We lived about seven miles from the doctor in the neighboring town. I didn't have to wait long to see him. He heard my cries in the waiting room.

I protested so loudly he decided not to put stitches in my knee. He cleaned out the wounds carefully. Stones got into the wound when the bike punctured the skin. He wrapped it up tightly. My skin was torn all along my knee cap. The doctor wrapped it so tightly it looked like a cast on my knee and I couldn't bend it at all. I wondered how I would look on stage. My dress would not be able to cover this big white wrapped knee.

The neighbor man drove me to school. The students were ready to practice for the program. We had to walk up the hill to the church building. The program was in the church basement. I had to limp slowly along.

I limped on to the stage the next night. Everyone could see my big bandage. They all heard the story. I loved telling about how LeAnne didn't come back to help me. Could the people tell, what a mean sister I have, I wondered?

I never knew I could get so much attention from an injury. It didn't seem so bad. Mama told me that it will be better before I get married.

RHUBARB COBBLER

3 1/2 cups cut up rhubarb
1/2 cup milk
1 3/4 cup sugar
3 Tablespoons butter
1 Tablespoon cornstarch
1 teaspoon baking powder
1 cup flour
1 cup water

Place rhubarb in bottom of 13 by 9 inch buttered baking pan.
Mix 3/4 cup sugar, add butter, flour, baking powder and milk.
Pour mixture over rhubarb.

Mix 1 cup sugar and cornstarch.
Sprinkle this mixture to cover batter.

Pour 1 cup water over all.
Bake at 350 degrees for 45 minutes.

Refreshing summer desert

GRANDPARENTS

My grandparents, my mother's parents, Charles and Louise, would come out to visit us in their black 1938 Buick. I remember it had vent holes in the side and a trunk with a shelf in it. I thought this was really special. I remember how excited I was on their arrival. They would bring us eggs from the farm and other treats that they had packed on the shelves in the trunk. My grandmother took out the eggs. None of them were broken.

My grandfather always had a silly rhyme for me. One of them went like this: "I love you with my heart, I love you with my liver; but if I had you in my mouth, I'd spit you in the river." He could say it over and over again and I wouldn't tire of it. My grandfather liked to give out silver dollars. We usually always got one for our birthdays and sometimes when he came out for a visit. I still have several of them. Sometimes I spent them to buy Christmas presents for my family.

My grandmother would help my mother in the house. Sometimes she did some mending, or would help my mother with canning the fresh vegetables. My grandfather would tell stories and play games with my brother and me. He liked to bounce us on his knees. He would make silly faces at us. He would give us hugs.

I loved to go and visit my grandparents who lived near my cousins on the farm. We usually went out on a Sunday afternoon. As the cows always needed milking my grandparents usually came to the farm when we visited and had dinner with us.

My cousin Elizabeth had four brothers. She was always trying to keep up with them. Her mother called her sister. I don't know why. Everyone else called her Elizabeth. Maybe she wanted her to be a sister to her, instead of a daughter. We were kindred spirits and always had a good time together.

She had lot of toys. She had a big bedroom all to herself. I had to share mine with my two sisters. There was a porch off her bedroom on the second floor. There was an attic that even a grown-up could stand up in. Their house also had a big enclosed front porch off the living room. I loved their big house. This was the house my mother had grown up in with my grandparents until she married my dad and moved to the city where he was a schoolteacher. After her brother married, my grandparents bought a new house in the nearby village. My grandfather continued to help his son Clarence on the farm for many years.

Beside the barn, there was the machine shed, the garage, the chicken house, the pig pen and the big garden. It was a big world to explore for a five-year-old girl. I loved going to the farm. I always had a good time. My Uncle Clarence was a big man and he had a big booming voice and smoked a cigar. I was a little bit afraid of him. He loved to tease me.

I especially loved to visit Elizabeth during threshing time. This was in August, my favorite month because it was my birthday month. My parents would drive to my uncle's farm to help him and the neighboring farmers with the haying. My mother would help Aunt Eleanor in the house to cook the two big meals every day for the threshers.

A few days before this my uncle and grandfather had cut down the oats in the field with the binder machine. It cut the oats and bundled it with a heavy piece of binder twine. Then my grandfather, or sometimes my grandmother, followed the binder machine and stood the shocks up to dry.

After the oats were cut down in the field and made into shocks, they were hauled into the barnyard. One or two of the farmers lifted the big shocks of oats and threw them into the threshing machine. The threshing machine was a huge piece of farm machinery. The threshing machine separated the oat seed from the stalk. It created lots of dust. The empty stalk came out one pipe and a big pile of straw was created. The seed from the oats was sent down another chute into a covered wagon and then hauled to the shed called the granary. There it would be stored for the winter until my uncle took it to the feed mill to be ground into mash to feed his cattle. Sometimes ground wheat or other food supplements would be added to the oats. This feed and hay were the main food for the cows during the long Wisconsin winters. Farmers who grew wheat also used the threshing machine to separate its seed from the stalk.

Meantime in the house, my mother and grandmother would be busy peeling potatoes to make the mounds and mounds of mashed potatoes needed to feed the hungry men from working the thresh machine all morning. Other farmers drove the wagon full of shocked oats. The young men took the big pitch forks and threw the oats up on the wagon. Everyone worked hard.

Each day my aunt baked fresh fruit pies. Chickens would have been killed and cleaned the night before to have fresh roasted chicken to eat. Beans or corn were picked in the early morning from the garden for a fresh cooked vegetable. My grandmother would have started to bake bread early in the morning. By noon time fresh bread would be coming out of the oven. The kitchen was filled with the aroma of freshly baked bread and fruit pies, and roast chicken. I was fascinated to watch the men eat the mountains of food. Thrashing was hard work for both the men and the women.

The day of threshing season I remember best was when I got hurt. Elizabeth had learned how to ride her big bike the summer before. I had just learned how to ride. They were much bigger than we were and very heavy. The bikes were fun to ride about on the farm. It never was a very smooth ride as few of the roads were paved. The hill up to the hay barn was worn smooth from the wagon tracks. It was packed down earth. The hill up to the hayloft was always fun because you could coast down with your hands up in the air.

Elizabeth had discovered a new trick with the threshing machine at her house. The threshing machine was very noisy. Our mothers were busy in the kitchen. The farmers were busy watching the machines. There were lots of pipes going this way and that. The various pipes separated the oats from the straw. The oats spewed out one end, and the straw at another end, making a very big pile. The pipe ran past the bottom of the hay barn hill.

With a head start at the top of the hill, Elizabeth could get her speed up and jump over the pipe. It was a neat trick. I watched her do it. I thought I could do anything that she did. I followed. I hadn't noticed the pipe connection sticking out above the pipe. It was too late to stop. I was going too fast. I hit the pipe where the connector poked out and tumbled forward.

I let out an awful scream. Even the threshing machine men heard me. They turned down the belts on the machine and they came running over to see what happened.

The main injury was right above my eye. I was bleeding terribly. I remember a big red dirty handkerchief coming down over my forehead. I don't know what frightened me more: the big threshing machine men trying to help me or my bloody forehead.

Momma, grandmother and Aunt Eleanor rushed out from the kitchen. My aunt said, "We need to take her to the doctor." I screamed louder, no. I didn't like doctors.

But, to the doctor I went.

My grandfather drove my mom and me. It was a nasty gash. The doctor cleaned out the wound and bandaged the area all around my eye. He gave me some candy. I enjoyed the candy. It is gone, but the scar can still be seen, but it is hidden by my eyebrow.

Another memory of that summer was getting a shock from the electric wire that kept the cows in the barnyard. Elizabeth and I talked about how much it would hurt.

I saw the scratches on my grandmother's arm where she had touched the wire. We dared each other to touch it. Luckily for us, Uncle Clarence had turned the power off and we didn't get hurt.

During hay season my parents stayed in the village about three miles away at my grandparent's house. I always begged to sleep at the farm. I liked visiting my grandparent's house, but I didn't like their bathroom faucets. They were black and they scared me.

One day my momma finally gave in and said I could stay at the farm for the night. I could sleep with Elizabeth in her bed. We were both very excited. My sisters had stayed there already, but this would be my first time all by myself. It took us a long time to fall asleep. We were both excited.

In the middle of the night I woke up. I couldn't remember where I was. I called for my momma. Everything looked strange. My crying woke up Elizabeth. I was scared. I cried louder. Soon Aunt Eleanor and Uncle Clarence were in the bedroom. I wanted my momma. They couldn't quiet me down, so at 3:30 AM Uncle Clarence had to drive me into the village to sleep at my grandparent's house where my momma was staying. I was so embarrassed. I didn't understand that it was okay at five years old to be scared sleeping in a different bed in a different house without your parents.

My grandmother always gave me special presents. The Christmas I was four she gave me some miniature china dishes. They were just like a grown-up set. They were in four colors: gold, blue, rose and gray. They had big four-inch plates and matching cups and saucers. My grandmother also gave me a set of plastic goblets for dessert and water. Another Christmas she gave me a set of blue plastic dishes with a tea pot and matching plastic silverware. One Christmas she bought pretty red velvet fabric that my momma sewed into new dresses for each of her daughters.

My grandmother had two daughters, but the oldest died when she was only thirteen in the flu epidemic of 1919. My momma told me about Clara, her older sister and what good pals they were. My momma was only nine years old at the time. She remembers that everyone in her family and neighborhood was sick. The doctor came but there wasn't any medicine that could take away the flu.

The local churches didn't even have separate funerals for everybody because so many were dying. It was a sad year.

The summer I turned five my grandmother died. I didn't understand. Nobody took time to explain to me what had happened. I went to the funeral home. I remember seeing my grandmother all laid out in a big box. There was a net over her face. Why did I touch her? Why was there a net over her face? Why didn't she talk to me? Children were to look, not ask questions. I asked my momma many years later about the net on my grandmother's face. She said it was there to keep the flies off, as it was a very warm day in the summer.

Everyone was going to church. It was not a Sunday. Did I want to go to church or stay with Elizabeth on the farm? I chose to play with Elizabeth. Why would I go to church when it wasn't even Sunday?

Years later I realized that it was my chance to say good-bye to my grandmother. I still feel sad, when somebody writes to me about a friend or relative's death. It doesn't give me the chance to say good-bye. That's important. I didn't get to say good bye to my dad. I don't want that to happen again.

My grandfather moved back to the farm after my grandmother died. The house in the village was sold. It was a pretty house. It had a big front porch and lots of trees. It was a warm and cozy house, except for the black faucets.

Now that my grandfather was alone my mother wanted me to write to my grandfather. I never knew what to say. I usually started, "How are you? I am fine." What else does a six-year-old say to her grandfather? But I kept writing him week after week. Sometimes he would come out to visit us in the country. It was a long drive for him. I knew the route back and forth to his house by heart.

My parents had a 1946 Chevrolet. After we left our country road we were on a national highway. Then we would have the turn where the big house was with the white fence. After that road we went through a town called Wrightstown. Then through the country village of Greenleaf. This was the place where my grandparents lived when they moved off the farm. It was the village where my momma went to school when she was a young girl. After we saw these landmarks I knew we were almost there. It was a gravel country road. After the hill you could see the barn and the farm house. Here at last! The farm was forty miles from our house. As there were no expressways, it took over an hour to get there

We continued going to the farm. Our whole family would drive out on a Sunday afternoon. I'm not sure how the visit was for my sisters as the cousins their age were boys. But we all got along with each other and really had a good time. I thought of Elizabeth as my best friend.

Our families visited back and forth for many years. Then I heard that she was going to have a baby! Oh no! I didn't know what was happening to my world. I knew you were supposed to be married to have a baby.

Elizabeth was only 16, the same age as me. I heard my parents talking about it in hushed voices. This was awful. They also heard that Elizabeth was getting married to an older man and she hadn't yet finished high school. My parents didn't know if he was Lutheran.

My parents were upset. My cousin Paul was planning to be a minister. How could Elizabeth do this to her family? Elizabeth and I had never written to each other. If I wrote her now, what would I say? I didn't know what to do.

My parents didn't talk about it with us children. My grandfather had died six years earlier. The visits to the farm were less and less often. Elizabeth moved far away and I was busy getting ready for college.

Some time later I went back to the farm to visit Elizabeth's youngest brother who now ran the farm. It was fun. It brought back a lot of memories. Elizabeth and I have gotten back in touch with each other. It would be fun to see each other again. I wonder if she remembers the day I fell off the bike? Or how we played up in the attic? I have many wonderful memories. I hope she does too.

I was so molded by the German church community I lived in. As a child I knew not to ask questions. I observed and wondered.

GRANDMA'S NUT BREAD

2 cups brown sugar
1 teaspoon salt
1 cup raisins
1 cup dates
1 cup chopped nuts
2 eggs
1 1/2 cups sour milk
Use vinegar or some lemon juice in sweet milk to sour it;
About one Tablespoon per cup milk
1 Tablespoon shortening
4 cups flour
1 teaspoon baking soda
2 Tablespoons Molasses

Mix all ingredients.
Hand stir.
Put in two loaf pans.
Let rise 20 minutes
Bake in slow over, 325 degrees for one hour
Test with a toothpick to see if done.

Favorite for Thanksgiving dinner.

COUNTRY LIVING

I think for my mother the hardest part of moving out to the country with her four young children was to go from having a modern house of the 1940's in the city to a house without indoor plumbing or central heating. I was only a baby of three weeks old when my dad moved his young family to the country.

In the city they had just left, my mother could walk to the grocery store or have my older brother and sister go and pick up some milk or other items needed. Her parents lived only twenty miles away.

My mother's parents lived over forty miles away and she couldn't drive a car. My mother felt very isolated. My dad was very busy setting up to teach all eight grades of school. My mother had to manage on her own with four children and in a few years five.

Even growing up on her dad's farm, my mother was used to indoor plumbing and some modern conveniences. This house did not even have hot and cold running water. There was a hand pump in the kitchen that drew water up from the cistern for washing the dishes. The drinking water had to be pumped up from the outside pump located in our back yard. My mother also had to heat the water to wash the clothes on the cook stove. It was a very difficult adjustment for my mother.

Not having indoor plumbing the first five years of my life, I can't remember thinking it was all that bad. It was just a part of life. Our outhouse was right next to the garage. It was a three holer. It had a shorter, smaller hole for us young ones and two larger, higher holes for the older children and adults. In place of the modern convenience toilet paper, a Sears catalog or other scrap paper was there for your use.

I know I didn't linger going to the outhouse. I remember that. At night, we were allowed to use an indoor chamber pot, or we would run out with a flashlight before we went to bed. After a few years using the outdoor facility the church committee decided to purchase a chemical toilet for our family. This was put down in our basement. I was terrified of it. It was big and black and made a terrible noise when it was flushed. It was placed right next to our big furnace that had just been installed. Nearby was the coal bin. I found all this very scary.

Also down the basement was the cistern. This was in the next room where there were shelves for the fruit and vegetables that my mother canned each summer. I knew that behind its wall was water. I was afraid I would somehow fall in and drown. That really was impossible, as the wall was over four feet high. My mother stored empty fruit jars on top of the wall and sometimes she would send me downstairs to bring some up for her when she was canning. She also kept her huge tin of old clothing scraps next to the cistern. It was always cool down there, as the walls were very thick.

And then the sump pump was put in. It was smelly and noisy. I was not sure what it was for, but on wash days my mother could empty her tubs of water onto the floor and it would go down the sump pump. It made a lot of noise.

The church members remodeled the house when I was about five years old. My brother was a baby. It was then that we got running water in the house, plus hot and cold water. No longer would my mother have to heat water on the cook stove on wash day. A bathroom was put in the room, which had been my dad's study. They enclosed the back porch and gave him a new study. They raised the roof of the upstairs attic to make a large bedroom for us three girls. A small storage area was built in the new entrance, which included a broom closet. The only difficulty was that the only way to enter this storage area was to climb up the shelves in the closet and fit through the small two foot by two foot opening.

I remember seeing a carpenter crawling in this storage area when it was being built. I expressed my fear to my mother that he wouldn't be able to get back out of such a small hole. Later, whenever I complained about having to put something in the storage area, my mother would remind me that I was the only one who could safely get in and out, except of course for my younger brother.

Wash day was fun. I liked to see the clothes go through the wringer. The first time the clothes would go through the wringer they were filled with soap. They would fall into a clothesbasket set on the floor. Then I could hand the clothes piece by piece to my mother and she would feed them one piece at a time through the wringer into the rinse water. The clothes were then swished around in the clean rinse water. After about ten minutes my mother would turn the agitator off. Now the clothes had to have their final time through the wringer. The clothes once again became all flattened and squished. The water ran back down into the tubs to be used over and over again. All the water was recycled over and over again. The white clothes were washed first. By the time the washing was finished the water was very dirty. While one load of clothes were washing my mother would then carry a completed load up the narrow basement steps and then outside to be hung on the clothes lines to dry.

We had five very long clothes lines and two shorter lines. There was always lots of laundry for a family of seven. In the winter, clothes were hung in the basement wherever and however my mother could find places to string a clothesline. Until the temperature dipped below freezing and there was snow on the ground, my mother hung the clothes outside.

Many times they would get very stiff from the cold. I could bend them and we would bring the clothes inside to thaw. As a child I had fun with my dad's long underwear. It looked so silly to me. My dad really did wear this strange contraption with flaps and buttons everywhere. My dad never did convert to modern boxer shorts or briefs. And until I went to high school my mother sewed all my underwear.

This was before the days of wash and wear!

At school we also had outhouses, one for the girls and one for the boys. My Dad tried and tried to get the church to build an indoor bathroom for us school children, but the stubborn old farmers held out. The women, of course, had no say in the matter.

As a student, I often ran out in the winter past the woodshed to the outhouse. I didn't linger! In the warmer weather though, I would take my time walking back to the schoolhouse.

The church property had outhouses up until 1968! The old ones were finally torn down, and the modern age moved in.

Stories can be told of the pranks played with the old outhouses. Halloween was an especially tough time for those houses. Farmer often found them in their front yard the next morning, or out in their cornfield.

Our outhouse toilet stood next to the garage. It was cold in the winter and infested with flies in the summer. Flies were everywhere in the summer, as the farm yards were right next door. One farmer had his cows and pigs practically in our garden. Another neighbor's sheep were just across the road, so what could we expect? Flies were everywhere.

As a child it was great fun to spray with DDT and watch the flies drop dead. Sometimes I would see how many I could swat dead in five minutes on the front porch with a flyswatter. Ten, twenty, fifty...zoom...bang...dead! My brother and I would compete as to who could kill the most flies.

For my mother of course it was often hard to see the thrill of living out in the country. Is it a wonder that when folks talk about the good old days, that forgotten are the long cold nights and days with the Sears catalog sitting on a hole? It was not the place to read or linger any longer than necessary. No way!

ZUCCHINI PICKLES

5 lbs. zucchini, thinly sliced
1/2 cup salt
Combine in large kettle and cover with ice.
Optional: add 3 medium onions on top of ice.
Let stand 3 hours.
Drain and rinse.

Combine the following in large sauce pan
3 cups vinegar
3 cups sugar
1 1/2 teaspoon turmeric
2 teaspoons celery seed
2 teaspoons mustard seed
1/2 teaspoon black pepper
1 teaspoon ground ginger

Heat to boiling.
Combine zucchini with mixture, bring to boil again.
Reduce heat and simmer 2 minutes.
Pack in glass jars and seal.
While hot, process in boiling water bath.
Makes 5 - 6 pints.

Great way to enjoy zucchini all winter long.

DOLLS

Most little girls have dolls and I was no exception. I remember Susie and Cherry. Then there was my very big special doll, Julie twenty-six inches tall. It's ironic that I chose those names, for when I got older, married, and had my own daughter, I chose Gretchen for her name, a much more substantial name. But I know as a young child I always liked names like Susie, Jill, Ann, Patty.

Most dolls, when purchased, only came with one set of clothes. Susie came in a blue and white checked dress, little panties to match and a hat. Cherry, I think, only wore a diaper, but she also had a baby bottle as she wet when she drank! Both dolls were only ten to twelve inches tall, but I loved them dearly.

My mother had a treadle sewing machine at that time and I watched her, fascinated for hours while she was sewing. The treadle would go up and down, up and down, back and forth. My mother made clothes for all of her five children, often from older clothes that people gave to her to make over the best she could. She sewed coats, jackets, dresses, curtains, hemmed towels, and even made our underwear. Sometimes she would let me pump the treadle machine. I was enchanted.

There were always lots of scraps of material around in all colors and all sizes. I saw her cut out the patterns, and saw how the sleeves fit into the armholes. I saw her put elastic in a waist band. It didn't look that hard. Why couldn't I do that?

I had not yet started school, as I was only five years old and no kindergarten program existed at that time. I made my own patterns out of tissue paper and laid them on the fabric. I cut them out and tried my hand at sewing. For some things it was extremely difficult to sew such little objects on the big machine, but it was very satisfying to me. My dolls had great outfits. I made diapers to match the dresses, sewed ruffles on the Sunday best outfits, made bonnets to match and lots of sundresses. These were the simplest as they didn't need sleeves.

I had the best dressed dolls in Wisconsin. A few of the outfits have survived to this day!

HEATH BARS

½ cup butter
½ cup shortening
Cream together shortening and butter
Add the next four ingredients:
1 egg
1 cup brown sugar
2 cups flour
1 teaspoon vanilla
Mix all ingredients together.
Spread on cookie sheet.
Bake at 350 for about 30 minutes.
Frost with chocolate chips (1 pkg.)
Lay whole chips on baked cookies, place in oven to melt.
Then spread the chocolate chips like frosting on the top.
Let cool and cut into squares.

Favorite for special luncheons.

PAPER DOLLS

Playing with dolls was always one of my most loved pastimes. I loved to live in a world of pretend. I loved to play dress-up. I would pretend I was married. I'd choose a famous ball player for my husband, and I would make up a complete fantasy world.

In addition to my baby doll, I loved playing with paper dolls. This was different. Here I would go into their world and be a grown-up, have a career, but not usually a Mom.

I had lots of different paper dolls through the years. They were often movie stars.

I had Esther Williams. I would pretend I was Esther, being not only a great swimmer, but also a movie star. I hardly ever went to the movies. My dad didn't approve of most of them and those on television were on past my bedtime. I could read about the movie stars in "Photoplay" magazine, or hear about them from my friends.

The paper dolls usually came in sets of two dolls, each with a different pose and hair style. I would pretend it was Esther's sister, or best friend.

I had Janet Leigh. She was so pretty. I would carefully cut out all the clothes that came with each doll. I would keep them in their original folders so that they wouldn't get lost. I usually played with the paper dolls outdoors in the summer under our willow tree. It provided shade, and it was away from the road. I wanted to be alone in my fantasy world.

Sometimes my friend Kathy from school would come over. She was an artist. She would design more clothes for my dolls. I would help color them and cut them out. A few times we chose dolls from the Sears Roebuck catalog. We would paste them onto some heavier paper so that they wouldn't be so flimsy. Then Kathy would draw clothes for these dolls.

Most of the paper dolls cost nineteen cents a package in those years. The price went up to twenty-nine cents, then thirty-five cents by the time I was in fifth grade. They were really getting expensive. I wasn't babysitting yet, so I had only the money I would earn from picking cucumbers.

Elizabeth Taylor cost 59 cents. She was so special. She came in an extra fancy cardboard cover. My mother gave me some money for chores so that I could buy her.

I was all excited when I found the Lennon Sisters. Then I found a nurse and a pilot. They made the perfect Cherry Ames and Wade Cooper, Cherry's boy friend. I relived the book *Cherry Ames, Army Nurse* over and over.

Soon I'd be too old to play with paper dolls. But it was such a nice world. People were polite; you didn't have to worry about hurt feelings, or being awkward or gangling. I could be a dancer as smooth as Fred Astaire and Ginger Rogers. It was a wonderful world and I wanted to hang on to it as long as possible.

FIVE-MINUTE FUDGE

Combine 2/3 cup undiluted evaporated milk with 1 2/3 cups sugar in saucepan;
Heat to boiling.
Cook five minutes, stirring constantly.
Remove from heat.

Cut up 16 marshmallows, 1/2 cup chopped walnuts and add to milk mixture.
Then quickly add 1and 1/2 cups semi-sweet chocolate bits and 1 teaspoon vanilla.
Stir until marshmallows are melted.
Pour into buttered 8 or 9 inch square pan.
Garnish with walnut halves.
Cool.
Cut in squares.

Quick and easy and fun to eat.

THE SWING

Every child should grow up with a long rope swing; a thick rope hung on a ten-foot high branch of an oak, maple, or in my case, a box elder tree. The rope would be knotted under a board. There is no better place on a warm summer afternoon than to be on a rope swing. I would have a pile of books and homemade cookies stacked on the side of the tree. If it were early in the spring, I would have to watch out for the box elder bugs, red and black creatures that hung around the base of the tree. They were harmless, but I never got the appetite to eat cookies covered with them!

The swing ritual went like this; I took a book and then pumped for a while to get a smooth rhythm going. The legs were stretched while your back laid way back; then the reverse motion, legs tucked underneath your body while leaning forward. I would go back and forth, over and over again until I was reaching up to the sky, back and forth, faster and faster. Then I would open the book and could swing back and forth, back and forth and enjoy the breeze as I read *Pollyanna* or *Cherry Ames*, *Clara Barton,* or *Girl of the Limberlost.* I was caught up in another world.

After a while when I would tire of going so slowly, I usually dropped the book, and started pumping really, really hard, trying to reach the tree branches with the tips of my toes. Then I would give a strong yank to the rope, to the right to start the rope twirling around and around. When I got the rope as tight as it could go, I would give it a strong yank to the left, tucked my legs under the board and I would be spinning round and around. Oh, the exhilarating feeling! Sometimes I'd repeat and do it the second time and then jump off the swing and see how dizzy I had become!

By then it was time to just sit quietly under the tree, eat a cookie or two and continue reading the story. In this manner a whole afternoon could easily be spent.

The school swing was fun, but it had a chain instead of a rope. I couldn't twirl the school swing. However, when I felt really daring, I would get a friend, hopefully an older boy who was stronger than me and have him hang onto the board and run under the swing. This sent me really flying high, almost even with the top bar of the swing set. By stretching out my long legs I could sometimes touch the tip of the nearby oak tree.

Another fun swing was the monkey bar. Sometimes I would just sit on the bar and swing, or when I was going quite fast I would drop down and hang by my knees. For a final effect, I would turn a backward summersault to get off!

Then there were the chain swings. These were two link chains about a foot apart, with a ring at the end to hold one's shoe. This was about five feet off the ground, so to get on it, I had to be an acrobat. I usually put my hands in the rings, and swung myself around. Then I could pull myself to a standing position. To get off, I would dangle by my feet and turn a backward summersault, or else just jump down. If I wasn't feeling daring, or wanted to rest, I would just sit on the balance bar, or try to walk across it. This was a one-inch tube bar, about six feet across, and about five feet off the ground. I could also use this to get to the top of the big swing bar and then slide down the anchor pole.

The younger children would usually be sliding down the slide, while the big "children" were busy showing off. Well, one time I suppose in a moment of "showing off" I slid down the big pole that anchored the whole swing set into the ground. I waved my arms gaily into the air. Then I lost control and twisted and turned to the inside side of the bar and, with that, banged the pole. WHAM! I knocked my new big front tooth against the pole. I was seven at the time. Sure enough, the pole was stronger than my new tooth and there, lying on the ground, was a chip off my tooth. To mark the place where I hit the pole, a chip of paint came off the pole that matched the new shape of my front tooth. Both the chipped pole and the chipped tooth remained for a long time to remind me of my day of glory...or was that my day of folly?

RAISED DOUGHNUTS

2 packages active dry yeast
1/2 cup sugar
1 cup warm water (not hot)
1 teaspoon salt
4 1/2 cups sifted flour
2 eggs
1/2 cup soft shortening

In mixing bowl, dissolve yeast in water.
Add half the flour, sugar, salt, eggs, and shortening.
Beat with spoon until smooth and batter falls from spoon in "sheets."
Using your hand, mix in enough of the remaining flour until dough cleans the bowl.
Turn out onto lightly floured board.
Cover and let rest 10 - 15 minutes.

Knead until smooth and blistered, about 10 minutes.
Place in greased bowl, turning once to bring greased side up.
Cover with cloth.
Let rise in warm place until double in bulk, about 2 hours.

Punch down; cover and let rise again until almost double in bulk, 30 to 45 minutes. Punch down; roll out 1/4 " thick on floured board.
Cut with floured 3" doughnut cutter.
Let rise on greased baking sheet until very light, 1 to 1 1/2 hours.
Leave uncovered so crust will form on dough.

Fry in deep hot fat (375 degrees) about ONE minute on EACH side or until delicately brown.
Drain on thick paper towels.
For sugared doughnuts; place in bag with granulated sugar, and shake.
Makes about 42 doughnuts.

Great on a cold winter evening.

UP THE ROAD

Up the road from our house was the minister's house. His name was Rev. Tornow. He served as the parish pastor for all the people that belonged to Zion Lutheran Church. He lived there with his wife and their five children. I liked Mrs. Tornow, the minister's wife, because she always smiled at me. She took the time to talk to me and didn't seem to mind if I visited her. So often after I called on Evelyn I would stop and visit with Mrs. Tornow. Their four oldest children were usually not home as they were away at college and their youngest daughter Elsbeth was in my Brother Lyle's high school class.

I never called a married woman by their first name. It was always Mrs. So and So. I knew Evelyn before she became married so she stayed Evelyn. What to call some of the older women who were not married was always a problem to me.

Were they called Miss Klemp or Miss Tews? Well, I was a Miss too, so that didn't seem right. Most of my friends could call these ladies Aunt So and So, but they weren't my aunts. I heard other grown-ups refer to them by their Christian name, Hilda or Eleanor. Dare I do that? Generally, I tried to avoid calling them by name. I would just start talking to them or smile shyly at them and they would talk to me first. I didn't have the nerve to say, excuse me Miss Tews. Why didn't they explain these things to a child?

I'm not sure what I talked to Mrs. Tornow about. She would ask me about my dolls, or my cats, or if I was getting excited about going to school. Her children were all older, so maybe that was why she didn't mind a young child underfoot. Perhaps I reminded her of when her children were younger. Sometimes I made cookies with her or she would have some paper for me to draw pictures on with crayons.

The Tornow's lived right next to the school, so sometimes I waited there until school was over and then would run over to see my Dad. That was the best time to see him. His teaching day was finished and he could relax a bit. He would let me help with some of the chores. I could help the other students who were assigned the after school duties. I could clean the erasers, wash the black board or put new picture on the bulletin board. Then we would walk home together. That's when I felt closest to my dad.

Sometimes he would let me stop and visit another neighbor on the way home. A new young couple was living in the big farmhouse across from the parsonage. They had a new baby.

The baby was so cute. This farm couple didn't seem as old as many of the other farmers. Their baby was the same age as my little brother so I knew how to talk to him. Then the mother would have to remind me it was time to go home. I knew to stay on the side of the road. I was a big girl. I had turned five.

SWEET PICKLES

1 gallon sliced cucumbers
1/2 cup salt

Ice overnight.

5 cups sugar
1 1/2 teaspoons turmeric
5 cups white vinegar
2 Tablespoons celery seed
2 Tablespoons mustard seeds

Empty all out into a large cooking pot.
Have it all come to a boil.
Put in jars.
Cover with sterilized lids.
Makes 6 - 7 pints.

Nice change of pace.

CHURCH

Zion Church was a tall yellow brick building with a high steeple sitting up on a hill. It was not a big hill, but long enough in the winter to go sled riding down the hill and sail for about a tenth of a mile. If it was slippery enough I could sail past the school house and with a little extra push would go on down the smaller school hill and then make it down to our house, "the teacherage," another tenth of a mile.

Of course I always had to watch for cars and then steer to the side of the road. But on slippery days in the winter, local people knew children would be out sled riding. No one ever got hurt, but when I was in the 7th grade, a school board member decided it was too dangerous and didn't want the school children sled riding during school recess or lunch hour. All of us children were upset, but he was on the Zion School Board, and so my dad, the teacher/principal had to enforce his ruling. That didn't rule out sledding after school, or Saturdays and Sunday afternoons.

In the other seasons, the church hill was great for bike riding. I never liked to pedal up the hill as these were the old regular coaster bikes. Once in a while I cheated and walked my bike up the hill, but never if anyone was watching! But once I made it to the top, checked out to see if any cars were coming, then whee! I would pedal for about six or seven turns, and then I could coast down the hill. I would put my hands up in the air and it would fly like I was flying. I could easily make it to the school house, pedal a bit more, and make it down the church hill and all the way home. Sometimes, the wind was against me, and then I had to settle for just a short ride. But the feeling of freedom as I breezed past the countryside was stupendous! Was there anything better in the world for a child to do?

When I was in high school, Zion church celebrated its 100th anniversary as a congregation. The yellow brick church built in 1885 stood on the highest hill in the area. All of my growing up years were spent attending Zion Church on Sunday mornings, and until high school I went to Zion School located just down the hill past the cemetery.

There were special events all year to help celebrate the 100th anniversary. The church booklet published for this occasion showed pictures of many of us who helped and were involved in the church activities at this time: Walther League society, Leadership Training, Missionary League, Men's Club and the church choir. The Walther League was the teenage group, named after one of the early Lutheran church leaders in America. The Leadership Training was a course that the pastor made some of us young teenagers take so that we would be better prepared to teach Sunday School.

The booklet has pictures from the early years, and the current years. In the background of one of the pictures was a bulletin board that I designed and put up. It had a picture of an open Bible, with a cross in the background. Words were cut out in big letters centered on the open Bible: "The fear of the Lord is the beginning of wisdom."

I remember that fear. I feared my dad. I feared the minister. I always heard what I should be doing. I was told that Jesus loves me, but Jesus and God didn't seem to be the same being.

Right across from the church lived Grandma Bartel. She always wore black. I never noticed her face. I just always saw this figure in black out in her yard, bent over.

The story is told about me when I was about three or four that I would say that I was going to see Jesus. My Mother always took this to mean that I was going up to the church where my Dad played the organ. He often practiced there on Saturday afternoons, or maybe after school. The church was just past the school and the church cemetery. I wanted to go see Jesus.

Well, I had been read Bible stories ever since I could remember and knew many of them by heart. The book was titled *101 Favorite Bible Stories.* I thought Grandma Bartel was Jesus. I never really noticed her in church, until one day. She always sat in the back corner of church, barely noticeable and she never stayed and talked to anyone. In later years I heard she was a bit crazy, but families didn't place their relatives in mental institutions so much in those days. Her husband took care of her.

But I didn't know at my age that she had a husband. I just thought she was Jesus. Then one day when I saw her, with my Mother next to me I said, "See, there's Jesus!" What a revelation to my Mother! And so the story went around. Louise thought Grandma Bartel was Jesus. Oh my embarrassment. How was I to know? She wore a long black dress like you saw in pictures of Jesus. Bible stories talked about seeing Jesus. He lived in the Church, so it was perfectly logical to my 4-year-old way of thinking.

I found out later, that she was the grandmother of one of my playmates. I still like to think that for a four-year-old, Jesus lived right across the road, tended His garden and came and sat in the back row of church on Sundays, just visiting, and not saying a word to anyone.

Church and spanking are two words that go together in my parochial school years. In church it was stand up, sit down, up and down, sit, sing, listen, and above all, do not talk! But how did you know what was going on? My friends were sitting in another pew. I couldn't even wave to them. The benches were hard. It was so difficult for me to sit so still. I wasn't supposed to write or draw. The only book I was allowed to look at was *The Lutheran Hymnal*. A hymnal was just a lot of words and musical notes. It was a book without any pictures, not even any Bible pictures.

The sermon was so long. The minister just talked and talked. Oh my, what was a child supposed to do? My oldest brother could sit upstairs in the balcony with his friends in the back row. My sisters could sit up front with the other school children in the front two pews, boys on one side, girls on the other side. I had to sit with my Mother and my baby brother. She was busy attending him and keeping him quiet. I was told many times by my dad that as his child, that was, the teacher's kid, I was suppose to set an example to the other children.

My Dad was upstairs on the organ bench, with a mirror. He could look down and see me and my Mother and the minister up front. The choir, which he directed, was sitting over to his left side. I had to sit quietly with my mother.

My friend Janice got to sit with both of her parents, as did Rogene and Joyce. I didn't think that was fair. I was always different.

Sometimes my Mother let me sit with Mrs. Tornow, the pastor's wife. She was usually sitting by herself. Her children were all grown up. I'm not sure why, but I liked sitting next to her. She liked me and I felt her warmth. But invariably after church, a full report would be given as to my behavior, and Louise was naughty again. I would get a spanking from my dad when I got home. He wanted me to sit perfectly still and not talk.

I remember sometimes I tried to hide in the back clothes closet, but of course I would be found. One of those times when I was hiding, I took my little scissors with me. I would teach my parents a lesson. If they thought I was so bad, I would be bad. I cut off my bangs! I cut them very very short. I got a spanking with the leather strap for that infamous deed.

But still through this all, I played church at home. I didn't spank my dolls though. I got them all baptized as I didn't want them to go to hell. Also, I baptized my cats, my friend's dolls, and sang the appropriate hymns. I knew it was okay if I baptized them for there was a page in the hymnbook that said a person could do the baptizing if a minister wasn't available. I sang the hymns, said the prayers, but I didn't preach sermons. I thought they were unnecessary. "Jesus loves me this I know, for the Bible tells me so, little ones to Him belong, they are weak, but He is strong." "Jesus Loves Me" was my favorite hymn for many years. I knew Jesus loved me, even if I was bad.

After church was the best fun. I could talk to my friends and run around. Everybody came out side and visited. It was the way to find out who was doing what and who did what on Saturday night. Everyone had their special place to stand. The school children stood in corner on the right side. The young teenage girls stood just down from the church steps in a circle. The young mothers stationed themselves a bit farther down the walk, in several clusters. The older women were usually divided by relatives as many of the members were related to each other. The older teenage boys stood in front of the church signboard. The men were over closer to the parking lot.

Everyone had their place, and if you needed to give someone a message, you knew which group they would be in and exactly where they could be found. The little children ran in and out and around the legs. Everyone stayed at least fifteen to twenty minutes after church just talking. There was never a coffee hour in those days. Coffee wasn't needed to entice people to stay. We all just stayed and visited. It was where I could find friends to go bike riding with that afternoon or if it looked like rain, to find a few friends to get together and play Monopoly. Once in a while somebody's Dad might be bowling and perhaps we could ride along and go to a Sunday matinee at the movie house.

Sometimes, in the winter some of the girls would go sit in a car and talk, but not usually. We all just wore heavy coats and mittens and stood outside in the cold winter air.

The Church Picnic was really special. This was always in the spring, usually the last Sunday in May. Children who had moved and grown up away would come back for it. A good home cooked dinner was served. Lots of homemade pie, cakes, salads, baked ham and chicken were served. Every family brought something to share. There was a bounty of good food to go around. And then the fun began. The school children were given tickets to purchase refreshments. School was now officially over for the summer. We could buy pop and candy at the stand. The stand was really a wood shed with doors that opened on two sides to reveal a counter. Candy corn, balloons and other trinkets were also sold, but pop was the big hit. We never had soda pop at home, just milk, milk, milk. This made pop a real treat at ten cents a bottle or two tickets.

After eating and buying a snack, most everyone would go down to the baseball field by the school and watch the older teenagers play either softball or volleyball. Sometimes, the older men played against the young men. Sometimes the young women teamed against men or teenagers with each other.

Before I started school I brought my doll and played house with the other young girls. When we got tired of our dolls we would go to the swing set and hang on the monkey bars, or run under the swing seat while another was on the swings, and see how high we could make it go. Once in a while, I could get my brother or another older boy to run under the swing and really let me swing high. Oh, it was such a wonderful free feeling to swing high up into the sky and touch the oak tree with my toe!

The cemetery was right there in the churchyard, and sometimes we would play hide and seek among the tombstones. Some of the older folks didn't like that, but what was the harm? The people were dead, they didn't care.

It was a fun day. If I got hungry in the middle of the afternoon, I could go down to the church basement, and some church lady would always give me some food. The older women were always busy cleaning up the kitchen. All the dishes had to be washed by hand. Paper plates, plastic forks were still not in use. There were always lots of leftovers from the noon dinner.

Supper was very informal. The men and women just went downstairs and had a sandwich, maybe another piece of pie and a cup of coffee. The children could go down and eat when they got hungry. The farmers would have to go home and do chores. The cows needed to be milked, even on church picnic days.

That way, I was lucky. I didn't have any pigs to feed or cows to milk. It was another way that made me different. It gave me more time to read books, one of my favorite pastimes.

BUNDT CHOCOLATE CAKE

Preheat over to 350 degrees
2 1/2 cups cake flour
1/2 cup powdered sugar
1 teaspoon baking soda
2 cups brown sugar
1 cup butter
3 eggs separated
1 teaspoon vanilla
1 cup milk
2 squares bitter chocolate and 2 - 3 heaping Tablespoons cocoa

Melt chocolate in small pan.
Separate eggs.
Cream butter, sugars, yolks and vanilla.
Beat
Sift flour with baking soda
Add chocolate and flour mixture with milk.
Lastly, beat egg whites and fold in easy.
Pour into well-buttered bundt pan.
Bake for 50 - 55 minutes.
Test with toothpick. If comes out clean cake is done.
Cool on rack.
Shake more powdered sugar over top.
Let rest a day.

Chocolate cake is always a treat.

ONE-ROOM SCHOOL

School... one-room… relics of the past... woodshed… outhouses... was this for real? Oh yes, very much so. Even more remarkable...of the five siblings in their grade school years, one through eight, 39 of those years, their father was their teacher! Unbelievable, you say, but oh so true. This could almost be called "home-schooling" by today's standards.

How was it? It was the single most important experience that has shaped me for life. To make it even more unique, this was you see a parochial school; not Catholic with a nun teaching, but a parochial Lutheran school. My father was the teacher. My dad, besides teaching his own children, taught 25 to 50 other children in any given year from the parish. It was very parochial. Outsiders were not permitted. Why not?

Well, who would come? Every day religion was taught from the Lutheran point of view. All other viewpoints were considered wrong or at least not as right as the Missouri Synod Lutheran way.

Now what is that you say? Well, it goes back to the Old Country. Germany generally is meant, but it could also refer to Norway or Sweden, maybe Denmark. All were European. There were very few English settlers in Wisconsin. The English were generally either Episcopalian or Methodist. In the Old Country many political upheavals were happening. Neighboring towns and districts were not getting along. Monarchs were setting the standard on church membership, and giving little if any freedom of speech. So, to the United States the settlers came, particularly in the mid-1800's. Each area of Europe brought groups of people, all with their way of looking at religion, church, doctrine, and traditions. Some settled in Missouri, others in Pennsylvania, still others in Wisconsin or Minnesota. Of course back in 1850 to1860 when the majority of these old churches came to their new country, the Protestant churches hadn't the years or centuries of getting established liked the Roman church, so thus local traditions and customs were developed from the era of the Protestant Reformation.

Thus it was that in different areas of the United States different Lutheran church groups emerged: Missouri Synod, Wisconsin Synod, Norwegian Synod and so on. Some sects merged or worked together as traveling preachers brought them together, or as in the case of Missouri Synod, some from that charter group moved to other areas of the country. Today the Lutherans still have synods. There have been mergers and cooperation has happened. But, in my school days cooperation was almost non-existent.

School days meant eight grades in one room. Some today see this as progress. Much can be said for it from the educational point of view, or from a child's point of view. No difficult transition from one room to the next. No new teacher to adapt to. No new rules to learn and very few new faces to learn. Except for the four or five first-graders, and these were often younger brothers and sisters of classmates, or a niece or nephew, or a neighbor's kid there were very few new children in the area. Most names were seen in the roll call year after year after year:

Tews, Drews, Krenke, Rochteschal, Klemp, Voight, Koch, Bruss, Schroeder are the family names that were in this region for many years. Today these names are still in the church roll, or on the newly named road signs that the county has put in place.

Here is a description of the school for those never having been inside a one-room school. First we have the entrance hall; here there is a shelf where we put our lunches. A child usually didn't have to put his name on the bag or lunch box as everyone knew everyone else's design or container. On really cold days in the winter, students were allowed to bring their lunches inside, as there wasn't any heat in the entrance hall and the students would freeze. The average high temperature in central Wisconsin in January was 25 degrees!

After the entrance hall you stepped into the classroom. First you saw the three sets of hanging clothes racks. The first rack was for the boys, with hangers for their jackets and a shelf for their caps. Next was the rack for the girls. In the winter the girls wore scarves and the boys wore ear muffs with their caps. The last rack was the small low rack for the first and second graders.

Also, in the back of the classroom was the wood burning stove. This was later upgraded to oil. Part of the teacher's duties was to get to school early enough in the morning to get the school house warm. It would have been dangerous to leave the fire going all night. It would also be difficult to stoke the fire hot enough to keep a fire for more than six to eight hours. Sometimes, the stove still had embers glowing in the morning, especially if there had been a night meeting.

Often in the winter, the water fountain for drinking froze and my dad would have to open the trap door and thaw out the pipe. He did this with a blow torch. Sometimes by just leaving the trap door open, the water pipe would thaw out after the stove got warmed up. In Wisconsin a drinking water fountain was called a bubbler.

I still can remember the morning when Janice came in from the cold and she leaned against the stove pipe. Janice had pretty red gold hair. It was done each morning in locks by her mother with winding the hair up in rags, round and round. It wasn't long before we smelled burning hair. YUK! She never caught on fire, but her hair got singed. What an awful smell. Mittens very often got too hot and would have to quickly be removed. The mittens were put on the top of the stove or on the pipes. This was in the day before waterproof mittens and children usually had the home-knitted variety. For warmth two or three pair were worn. They were usually knitted out of wool yarn. Mittens are much warmer than gloves as your fingers can keep each other warm, in addition to the wool coziness.

Next to the bubbler was a sink for washing hands. The sink and fountain were new when I started first grade in 1950. When my dad became teacher there in 1944, only a hand pump fountain was inside the classroom. No indoor plumbing was ever in the school.

Then came the rows of desks. The desks were on runners, usually four or five desks together. There were shorter and smaller desks for the younger grades. The runners were simply long slabs of wood, approximately four inches wide by eight feet long, that the iron legs of the desks were attached to with bolts. All together the school had five or six rows of desks.

Each night after school two students had to stay to sweep the floor, and another student to clean the blackboard, wash the sink, pound the erasers and empty the pencil sharpeners.

There were two pencil sharpeners in the school, one in the front near the teacher's desk, and the other in the back near the water fountain. In the days before the oil burner, all the paper and other burnable products could just be thrown into the classroom stove.

Even in later years, a wood burning stove stayed in the instruction room. There was very little trash that had to be taken outside to the big trash can. The other after school chore was to fill the wood box. In the middle of winter this had to be done more than once a day, and it was often given as a punishment for some misdeed done during the day!

Each week too, the rows of desks were moved, so that the floor wore evenly. This also meant, when you were in 7th or 8th grade, you would have a desk against the wall, a real honor.

This was neat as you could sit sideways in your seat, and lean against the wall, thus not having to sit up straight all day. It really showed at a glance who the big shots were.

The seats in the middle of this row had a storage shelf, and above it several big storage cupboards, where the music books, or extra paper and textbooks would be kept. You, as an older student, may have been put in charge of their distribution. The fun part of the cupboard was that there were doors on the other side that opening up into the instruction room. So if a friend was in the instruction room a student could pass a message or food through the double set of doors. Doors had to be slid quietly open, the arm quickly put through with a quiet knock, then hopefully the door opened on the other side and your message or food was delivered and went unnoticed by the teacher!

The teacher's desk was up front. My dad though did not teach sitting down. He was usually up and about, moving from front to back, row to row among the students. There was an inkwell in the front of his desk to fill up your fountain pen. Up front also, was a big bench with a seat that folded up. This was called the reading bench. Usually just the younger grade students came up to this bench for reading, but occasionally also the 6th, 7th and even 8th graders took their turn sitting on the bench.

I sat there holding my reader, with nothing around to distract me. At my desk, when I should have been listening to the story, I often played around, or colored while other students were reading… A lot of oral reading was done, one student after another.

Words were to be looked up in the dictionary, and written out with their definitions. Often a synopsis of the story had to be written out also. Some readers had workbooks, mainly in the primary grades, but generally my dad created assignments to go with each lesson.

Up front near my dad's desk, was a magazine rack and a table. We got a few subscriptions to magazines. "My Chum" was one of my favorites. It contained stories and the names and addresses of children from around the country. I made several pen pals from these lists. I could sit up there and look at magazines, or draw or write, if my work was finished. For many children, these were the only magazines they had. The school subscribed to "Life," "Saturday Evening Post" and "National Geographic." My dad was a prolific reader so we had lots of books and magazines at home including every issue of the "Reader's Digest" since 1934.

The other room, or its correct name, the Instruction room was added on after the initial one-room, so that the minister could come over and instruct the older students for confirmation.

Three times a week for an hour and a half the minister drilled the students in *Luther's Small Catechism*. This is a book that Martin Luther developed in the 16th century to help teach the basic teachings of the Lutheran church: the Ten Commandments, the Sacrament of Baptism, and the Sacrament of the Altar, the Creeds and the Confession. After the basic doctrines are listed,

Luther explained their basic meaning in a question and answer format, always followed with several Bible verses to show how the doctrine came from the Bible.

By the time I had two years of instruction I knew most of *Luther's Small Catechism* book by heart. This was important because on Examination Sunday the pastor could ask any question from the book and I had to know the answer. I trembled.

It was a very scary experience. I didn't want to embarrass my family. I didn't want to be the only child that didn't know the answers. Examination Sunday was always a very long church service. The 8th graders would sit up front in chairs, just down from the altar. The minister still had his sermon, and extra hymns were all sung. In fact, the students on trial also were expected to sing a hymn by themselves. The service usually lasted over two hours! Afterwards you celebrated.

Our family was usually invited over to some of the student's houses. Usually one family for dinner and another family for supper. The next week being confirmation Sunday, we would be invited to the remaining of the class for a special dinner or supper. If the class had more than four students, we went over in the evening, or perhaps the following Sunday, which was Easter.

Confirmation was always on Palm Sunday, the beginning of Holy Week in the church year. This tradition got started, because then the Confirmation Class could have their First Communion on Maundy Thursday. That was the day in Holy Week when Jesus first gave the Sacrament of the Altar, or the Last Supper to his disciples.

In later years this practice changed somewhat as younger parents objected to the rigors and humiliation that could occur in front of the entire congregation. The Examination was held on a Friday evening before Confirmation and only the parents, godparents, and church council members were invited.

While I was in grade school, the minister also instructed the younger students in Bible verses. My father would use this time to teach social studies or history of the church to the 7th and 8th graders in the Instruction room.

Learning Bible verses was simply called memory work. It was my downfall. I just couldn't get the words down in my memory bank. My mother would drill and drill me. I knew the Bible stories. I knew the meaning of the verses, but word by word was impossible.

The pastor had a little black book with all our names carefully printed in it. Next to it would be the chapter and verse of our memory work. If we missed one word, he would deduct five points from 100, and on down the list. Sixty-five was considered failing. That was a disgrace. I never got 65, but I often got 85 or 90. I was supposed to get 100. I was the teacher's daughter!

My dad expected memory work of us also, but didn't judge word by word that I recall. His toughest memory assignment was learning hymn verses. Every Friday afternoon we would have a hymn that we were to have learned. First and second graders need learn only a verse, 3rd and 4th graders two verses and so on. But the hymn was sung often during the week and came easier to me. I still remember the humiliation when a new girl in third grade came and had learned all five verses of the hymn "My Faith Look up to Thee." I had been happy learning two verses up until then!

After a few years the ordeal got easier and I learned tricks in memorizing. It never was my favorite thing to do. Later on, when I went to a Lutheran teacher's college and had to memorize two hundred Bible verses for a doctrine class, I was in a panic.

Soon I realized I was way ahead of most of the students who had gone to public schools. Where it became confusing was when the different editions of the Bible were used and I had to remember to say, "forgive our debts" rather than "forgive our trespasses," or "The Lord is my shepherd; I have everything I need," rather than "The Lord is my shepherd; I shall not want."

I still find the words I learned in my first years at grade school as the ones that come most readily to mind.

After the minister left at 10:30 AM, the Instruction room became the study hall for the older students. If you behaved you could use it to work on a project with someone, or you would be asked to help a younger student with some arithmetic problems or you could spread out on the teacher's desk and do a special art project.

One winter, my older brother built some ping pong tables for the Walther Leaguers. This was the church's name for its teenage young group. It was named after an early founder of the church. The ping pong table got stored in the Instruction room for the Walther Leaguers to use on their meeting nights.

Once in a while, my dad allowed us younger students to push the desks aside during the noon hour and we could hold ping pong matches. We had our favorite players and there was probably as much cheering as there was playing.

Sometimes on Sundays the Walther Leaguers met there and the young children could come and watch. I realize now, that I don't ever remember the school being locked. I don't even think there was a key for it. It just wasn't needed. Robberies or vandalism didn't occur and what would a person find in a school? Books, paper, pencils, not much of value that a robber could resell or use.

On the left side of the classroom opposite the two-way storage shelf was the library. This was a big bookcase, reaching from the floor to the ceiling. It held over five-hundred books.

The older students took turns being the librarian. A student could check books out once-a-week to take home. However, when your school work was done, a student could come over to the library anytime and read a book. We had all sorts of books. *Hardy Boys* and *Nancy Drew Mysteries* were everybody's favorites. I also enjoyed *Cherry Ames Nurse Stories* and pretended I would grow up to be an army nurse and marry a pilot. I also enjoyed reading the classics like Washington Irving's *Sketch Book,* and_*Quo Vadis,* and *The Big Fisherman,* by Lloyd C. Douglas. *The Bumper Book*, a collection of stories compiled by Wally Piper was my favorite in first grade. There were some Bible story books, but not very many that I recall. By the time I graduated in 8th grade I had read almost every book in the library.

Out in the school yard there were the bike racks as most of the students rode their bikes to school. Only the Posselts were driven to school on a regular basis and they lived about five miles away; the Hoewisch children were also driven to school in a car as they lived on a busy highway. In winter, a few more children got rides, especially the younger students.

The woodshed would today be called a storage shed. It was there basically to store wood and coal for the two stoves. But as winter wore on and the coal and wood got burned up, the woodshed was a great hideout for playing Cops and Robbers. It became the jail or sometimes the secret hideaway for the girls away from the boys. It was whatever your imagination made it.

On either side of the woodshed were the outhouses: on the left was the girls, on the right side the boys. First there was a protecting wall, so if a girl was in the house another student could wait there. It was a two-holer, so sometimes you shared, but usually not.

The boys had a trench and only used the house for number two. Those were the code words everybody used. I never heard the scientific words used for urine, or a bowel movement. Nor, did I hear any other slang words used. It was always #1 or # 2! During school, if a student needed to use the toilet they held up their fingers, one or two. The teacher would nod his head. Why a student had to indicate one or two I really don't know. Maybe so the teacher would know how long a student would be gone!

I never questioned the practice.

In the winter a student didn't ask permission to use the outhouse unless it was absolutely necessary; heaters were not provided. However, in the nice weather, students would be tempted to visit the outhouse for a chance to walk outside.

More stories could be told, of recess, long winter days, arithmetic games and on and on. My dad loved to teach. My father felt it was important for us to commit poetry to memory. He especially loved the narrative of "Evangeline" by Longfellow.

He didn't require the students to memorize the whole long narrative poem, only the first page or two. In addition, we each would have to write our own narrative of the story, illustrate a few of the key moments in the narrative, and choose twenty words that were new to us in the poem. Then we were to write out their definitions and use them in a sentence. This then would make up our "Evangeline" booklet.

My father loved booklets. We made ABC booklets in the first grade, geography booklets in the third grade, penmanship booklets, and science booklets. All aspects of a topic were put together in a format around a central theme.

I remember having to find five natural fabrics and five man-made fabrics, and tell where they came from and illustrate how they were used. I remember this particular assignment because of the trick my sister played on me.

I was gathering my fabrics. I had wool and cotton, a piece of silk and some leather, but I couldn't come up with a fifth natural fiber. And then I thought of rubber. We had rubber boots, so I thought that would be acceptable.

Where to find the rubber? I couldn't cut up my boots. Oh, but then I remembered there were old inner tubes in the garage. I could cut a piece from one of them. It was winter. It was already dark outside.

The path out to the garage was dark. There was a light switch once you got out there, but, it was about two-hundred feet from the house. It was long enough to be scary.

My sister said I was chicken. I thought I could wait until morning. But I was always rushed in the morning. Was I a chicken? Was I really scared of the dark? I'd show her. So, out to the garage I ran. I turned on the light and found the corner where the old inner tubes were stored. I cut a chuck of an inner tube and hurried out of there.

As I turned off the light, I thought I heard a noise. It was probably only an owl. I was about to run up to the house, and, "Boo!" My sister jumped out in front of me screaming!

I must have jumped 50 feet! "Ha! Ha! Ha!" She fooled me. Oh, what fun! I took off after her, but of course she was faster.

Oh, Louise, how silly you are to let LeAnne fool you. Just wait, I'd get back at her. Someday I hoped I could scare her and not be the little scared sister.

Child psychology, educational psychology, parent effectiveness training, these terms were not in the vocabulary back then. There were slow students and fast students. Some students were good in arithmetic, others were better in penmanship. Students knew each other's differences and accepted it. Parents didn't analyze it. We were all friends and visited in each others homes. Teasing and bullying were not absent, but it was not vindictive.

The toughest part was leaving the small grade school and going out into the big wide world of the public high school. It meant an hour bus ride each way. I was going to go from a class of four to a class of 144!

The one-room school house filled a very particular void for education at a time in our country's history. It gave an opportunity to children living out in rural areas a chance to learn and mingle with other children. It was a mixture of personalities and ideas. It opened the door for me to learn of the world outside of my country surroundings. It was a fascinating and unique experience.

COPPER PENNIES

2 lbs. carrots, cooked without salt; sliced like pennies
Onions, chopped, ¼ cup
Celery, chopped, ½ cup
Green peppers, chopped, ¼ cup
1 can tomato soup
1/4 cup salad oil.
Dash pepper.
3/4 cup sugar
1/4 cup vinegar
1 teaspoon salt
1/4 teaspoon Worchester sauce

Mix all ingredients.
Pour over carrots.
Chill overnight.

Nice summer salad.

LETTERS

July 4, 1979

Dear Louise,

I had Dad all eight years of grade school. During the 7th and 8th grades we had confirmation instructions for about 1 1/5 hours each day (the minister taught confirmation). These two years we had three pastors teaching instructions, due to pastors leaving.

I never really encountered problems with other members of the class because my Dad was the teacher.*

When I was going to school I think the teaching techniques were different then they are today. The same is true as far as our relationship at home. The teacher asked questions that had a direct answer. Where today more encouragement is given to open discussion and come to a conclusion. When I was in school it was teacher--student, teacher--student. Today we hope to have teacher - student - student - teacher.

I think the same principle carries over to the home. Rather than just say, this is it, throw out some points and lead to a common answer. When I started high school the same principle just continued on, so I had no problems with the teachers. I really think this new approach of teaching and relating is much better.

All in all, I don't think that the fact that I had Dad for a teacher for eight years really had an effect on me or our relationship at home. I think that Dad knew how to handle the situation he had in school real well. I never heard any negative remarks about it.

Have you heard about Effectiveness Training for Lutherans? A.A.L.** supports this program. It is 24 hours of sessions in which people learn the technique of active listening and relating. I haven't taken the course but have learned a lot about it.

Hope I have been a little help to you.

We are planning to leave for Wisconsin July 12 (PM) for vacation.

Love, Lyle

* Lyle was the oldest of the five children. His first 5 years of school were in a small city about 30 miles from this rural school. I was a baby (the fourth child) when my parents moved to the country.

**Lutheran fraternal insurance company that does a lot of community related projects.

[From my mother]

July 17, 1979

Dear Louise,

I suppose I better get my mind a working and answer your request about your Father being your Dad and teacher. It will be interesting reading the different views of each of you.

I do not think that having your Dad as a teacher changed the father/daughter relationship between the two of you. I'm certain being with him in school all day and then at home you got to know him better by spending a few hours with him each evening and week-end. You knew him at work and also relaxed at home if he ever relaxed.

I always was under the impression that your Dad treated his children like any one else in school - only expecting you to behave better. He probably would have helped you with your homework if he didn't have you in school. His common remarks were, "I explained it in school," or "I told you already what to do." (This made you angry.) When you were in the upper grades he depended upon you to help him correct papers and expected you (you worked together) knew your lessons. Sometimes I thought that Dad expected too much of you. I think Loren [1] had it the hardest in school with his Dad because Dad's nerves were getting very edgy. I remember you coming home and complaining about Dad expecting this or that. You loved to go to school and never wanted to stay home, even if you were sick.

When you were five years old, you wanted to attend school and one day in early fall, I asked you to go in our garden and pick up a few potatoes for our dinner. I don't remember if we had some dug or if you were supposed to pull up the plant. But instead of going to the garden, you ran to school--knocked on the door saying, "Daddy, leave me in." Daddy left you in.

Of course I started hunting for you. I even went to Arnold Klemps and Voights (neighbors across the road). Then Leone Rochteschel [2] called (on the telephone) that she saw you running to school. This was about 11:30 A.M. I don't recall if I walked to school or if Leone checked (to make certain you were there.) Leone was very young.

Another time when you wanted to visit school, I told you that you had to be quiet in school. When you came home, you told me that you were quiet, but Daddy talked all the time!

I often wonder how it would have been if you would have had someone else as a teacher in your early years.

I think it would have been easier on me if you had another teacher because I could never complain about things if I didn't agree with them. Oh yes, I complained and grumbled, but it didn't do any good. Your Dad taught you good studying habits because after we left Zion [3] the Superintendent of New London High School (wrote your Dad) a letter telling of the good working habits the pupils had coming from Zion and praised your Dad for sending so many outstanding pupils to N.L. I looked for the letter but I can't find it tonight. I know I have the letter someplace. Pastor Lucht printed it in the bulletin.

I'm not rewriting this--doubt if it will be of any help.

Hope you had a great time with Loren & Anita [4] and everyone in Philly.

Carri is still a problem. [5]

Lyle & Marlene, Paul & Mark left for Wis. [6] today. Carri and I will be leaving 3 weeks from today.

Lots of love to all,

Mother

PS GOOD LUCK

1 Loren was the youngest of the five children. He was five years behind me in school.

2 There was no telephone in the school. Leone was another neighbor who lived near school.

3 The name of the school was Zion Evangelical Lutheran School. My parents moved from Zion in 1965 and three years later the school closed.

4 I was living in Vermont at this time, and my brother and his wife had just recently moved back to Wisconsin after living five years in Oregon and we hadn't seen each other for over six years.

5 A granddaughter, being a teenager.

6 Lyle is the older brother, who moved with his wife Marlene from Wisconsin to Arizona while I was still in high school. Paul and Mark are sons of Lyle and Marlene.

I had written and asked my mother and my siblings on what they remembered or how they felt having their dad as a teacher. I was writing a paper for an Educational Psychology class. We were asked to write about something that we remembered happening during our school years that we felt had an impact on us either as a child or as an adult.

I wrote a paper on the spanking that my dad gave me in the seventh grade. The most memorable and I feel psychological damage I received from having my dad as a teacher was the spanking I received in front of all the school children when I was in 7th grade. This was the reason I had asked my siblings and mother for their letters to help me gain some added insight on having my dad as my teacher.

Briefly the episode that happened was this:

I always had to bicycle or walk home for lunch. I really wanted to stay with the other school children who were allowed to bring their lunch from home. On nice days they could even eat outside. They received a half-pint of either chocolate or white milk. I felt left out, but my dad was adamant about me going home for lunch. His reasoning was that "I have enough children to watch."

After much begging, my mother finally decided what harm could it do and gave me a lunch in a brown school bag. I put it in the hallway with the other school lunches. When it was time to have lunch that day, I went with the other children, got my lunch and went to my desk. When my dad saw that I had brought my lunch, he was very angry.

He demanded to know, "Why had I disobeyed him?" I probably said something, like, "I wanted to eat at school with the other children." With that he grabbed me out of my seat, took me over his knee and whacked me severely with a hard ruler. I was wearing a dress that day also, which made it doubly embarrassing.

I don't remember much after that. I think I ran into the other Instruction Room and cried. I was so humiliated. Many years later at a high school reunion talking to a grade school classmate, she remembered the incident well. She said how sorry everyone felt for me. But that they couldn't say anything to me, otherwise they would get into trouble.

I don't think I every talked to anyone about it. I was so embarrassed about it. Now I realized how much it would have helped to talk about it, and to know that the other students really sympathized with me.

I don't remember discussing it every with my dad. Maybe if he had lived longer that could have happened. He died in 1971, 8 months after my first child was born. I was 26 years old and had been a Lutheran school teacher for five years.

SLICED PICKLES

5 cups cider vinegar
1/8 cloves ground
5 cups sugar
4 large green peppers
2 teaspoon mustard seeds
10 large white onions
1 teaspoon turmeric
1/2 cup salt
2 teaspoons celery seed
50 medium size cucumbers

Wash cucumbers and slice thin. Chop onion and peppers finely.
Combine these with the cucumbers and salt.
Let stand 3 1/2 hrs. and drain.
Combine vinegar, sugar and spices in large preserving kettle.
Bring to a boil.
Add drained cucumbers.
Heat thoroughly, but do not boil.
Pack while hot into sterilized jars and seal.
Makes 5 quarts

Serve with melted cheese sandwich.

PENMANSHIP

Contrary to what is taught today, my dad, as my schoolteacher, felt that cursive writing should come before manuscript.

Now in teaching children to read, it does seem logical to learn manuscript first, rather than cursive, but my dad was adamant in his determination that cursive needed to come first. I can only think of it, like a baby learning how to crawl, before they walk. It may be related to development, as I don't think any of us children suffered on account of it, and maybe even benefited. In fact, my dad had very little use for manuscript, although he did have his students learn it. But first came cursive or both methods were taught at the same time.

Every day for fifteen minutes, his students would have Penmanship Studies. My dad would draw the special lines on the board with a music ledger. Skinny space in the center, maybe a quarter of an inch wide, a bigger space beneath and also above the skinny space, which was about 3/8 inches wide. Then a sentence would go on the board. We would start with a sentence using words, like Ann ate an awful lot of apples. **A A a a**. This we would have to write ten times. Then we would be told to write down 10 **a** words, or 10 towns starting with an **a**, or 10 Bible words, like **A**braham, **a**rk and on and on. The next day we would do **b**. **B**illy broke **B**ob's bicycle. **B b B b**.

The papers were then handed in. If the slant wasn't right, the correct Palmer penmanship method, this was noted, with his red pencil. If the letter tail wasn't long enough on a **g** or on a **y**, this was circled. I had to remember that the **t** wasn't as tall as the **l** or the **h**!

The penmanship exercise was for the whole school, grades 1 to 8. Of course, he didn't expect the young student to be as neat as the older students; but everyone had to do it, day in and day out. We kept our papers in a folder, and when we were done with the entire alphabet, we would make a special cover for it, and it became our *Penmanship Notebook.* I still have several of mine today.

I prefer writing to printing, but now after teaching primary grades the manuscript method and doing many manuscript stories for my younger students, I find myself doing a combination of cursive and manuscript styles.

Sometimes my dad would submit our papers to a Palmer contest and all of his students were proud to receive a certificate for good penmanship. I read not to long ago of an educator touring throughout the United States promoting the Palmer method.

The rebirth of calligraphy as an art form also says much, for a person's need to express himself with a writing style. Handwriting analysis is also now a popular activity. I wonder what my dad would think of it. He thought all our writing should be exactly as the textbook sample.

The other quirk of my dad's penmanship methodology was that he preferred the old or German **R**. It is unique. It starts off like a small hill, then a straight line up, and then a loop at the end. In later grades, my little rebellion would be to use the new or English standard cursive **r**. Today again I use a combination.

My dad also liked to use the German **t** which you didn't have to cross. It could only be used when **t** was at the end of a word. It is made by having a straight line up and then a hook. I often still make this **t** as it saves crossing time!

Does it matter? How important is good penmanship? Today your importance may be judged by how sloppily you write. I remember my son saying to me after I commented on how sloppy his handwriting had become, after having been so very neat when he was younger, he said, "I am practicing for when I become a doctor."

SPINACH SALAD

1 lb. fresh spinach
In blender mix:
¼ cup sugar
¼ cup vinegar
½ teaspoon dry mustard
½ teaspoon salt
1 Tablespoon poppy seeds
½ cup salad oil

To enhance, add some of the following:
Mandarin orange slices
Walnuts or pecans
Sliced strawberries

Healthy and simply delicious.

THE SKUNK

Seeing a skunk now and then was not so unusual when you lived out in the country. They were around, as was an occasional fox, raccoon or jack rabbit. They weren't usually seen around the house though, but off in the big woods.

None of these animals really bothered us. Some of the farmers got more concerned if they came in and bothered their livestock. Generally it was a live and let live attitude.

But, a skunk was a different matter!

It all happened the day before school was to open that fall. I had just turned 12 years old.

I was always excited the night before school started. My mother had sewed me a new dress, dark red with black figures in it, and the new dropped waistline, the princess look. I was moving up a grade and would be allowed in the confirmation room now, along with the other 7th graders and the all-important 8th graders. More privileges would come and the underlings really thought you were something. And it'd be fun to see all the children again. While you saw most of them in church on Sundays, you didn't get a chance to play with them. Most of the farm children had been busy all summer helping their parents run the farm. I was filled with anticipation. It was hard to get to sleep.

And then towards morning our dog started barking. Spotty didn't usually bark at night. He was tied up in back of the garage by his doghouse. But he sure was barking. Loud enough to wake up the neighbors probably.

By the time I went downstairs my mother was there already in her pajamas, along with my dad in his long nightgown. My dad didn't like pajamas; and my mother wouldn't wear nightgowns. I don't think either of them owned a bathrobe. My parents didn't usually walk around the house in their nightwear that was for the bedroom.

Well, by now, both my parents were talking excitedly. What was up? Hollering out to Spotty wasn't calming him down. Something was out there. And then we knew. The scent that was coming up to the house was a skunk.

My dad didn't own a gun, so he grabbed a shovel from the basement steps. And then all three of us were walking down the sidewalk to the house and we saw it. A very big fat skunk. Yuck! What a smell?

Why didn't the skunk run when we hollered? Poor Spotty, he was going around in circles on his chain. He couldn't get at the skunk and we couldn't untie Spotty for fear of the skunk. The skunk seemed almost tame.

And then almost instinctively I knew. He was a rabid skunk. He could bite. He could really hurt us and maybe he had already bitten Spotty. When the skunk saw us, he started toward us. We ran back up closer to the house. The skunk was near the back door. We had to keep running. So around the house we all fled... my dad, my mother and me. The front screen door was hooked so we kept running. And then with the skunk right behind us we made it into the house and just it time. The scent was unbearable.

Now the skunk was just standing there. My mother decided she'd have to call Melvin, the neighboring farmer, as he had a rifle. It was nearly time for him to get up anyway to milk his cows.

Ring, ring, we were on an old country party line. You turned the crank on the side of the telephone for whomever you needed. Melvin's ring was two even rings. All fourteen families on the party line could hear it ring. The telephone didn't usually ring at 5 A.M., so this would wake the whole countryside. Within minutes everyone would know about our skunk. With a party line, a newspaper wasn't needed for local news.

Ring, ring, where was Melvin? Crank it again for two more even rings. A long and a short ring would be for a different neighbor. Everyone knew everybody else's signal.

A sleepy "Hello" answered finally. Oh yes, he had his rifle. He'd load it and be right down.

Melvin came within ten minutes in his red pick-up truck. The skunk, a big fat old tom, was sitting three feet from our back door. He needed to kill him with one shot or another spray of his scent would permeate the house and probably us as well.

Boom! Bang! The skunk tumbled over dead.

Oh, yea! What a relief! And oh, my, what an odor!

The proper thank you was given out. The full story was related. Melvin said he had to leave to start his morning chores if my dad was sure he didn't mind doing the final burial. Not too many years before, Melvin had been one of my dad's students. He was glad to help out his teacher.

My dad, still in his nightshirt, pulled on some pants, took the shovel and then scooped up the skunk. He carried it out to the cornfield and dug a sizeable hole. Dad completely covered the hole then with cornhusks.

Poor Scotty, he was exhausted. The trouble was we didn't want to get near him. He really stunk.

My mother was afraid he might have been bitten. Without a close examination we couldn't tell. There were no obvious wounds on him. But, as a precaution, my mother would not let us go near the dog except to feed him for the next several weeks.

There was no thought of calling a veterinarian. We were allowed pets, but they were not allowed to cost extra money. Feeding and caring for five children was all my parents could afford. Needless to say, no one went back to sleep that night. Later on, the skunk story was told again and again.

My mother thought my dad should get a gun, but my dad refused. Once my older brother had been given a toy gun and my dad hid it and it was never found again. He had mellowed a bit though, for he allowed my younger brother to have a cap gun and holster set.

In later years, I heard that skunks made good pets. I think I would always be afraid that somebody would forget or not know which sac to remove, and wow, the scent of it all!

NUT HORNS

6 cups flour
2 cups shortening
1 teaspoon salt
2 Tablespoons sugar
1 package dry yeast
1 cup warm mild
4 eggs, beaten

In a large bowl measure flour, salt and sugar.
Cut in shortening thoroughly (as if making pie dough).
Dissolve yeast into the 1 cup warm milk; add to flour mixture.
Mix with spoon.
Then add the 4 beaten eggs. keep mixing dough.
Add a bit more flour if dough is sticky.
Use hands to mix dough into large ball.
Cover with towel or wax paper and let sit until you make the filling.

FILLING

2 lbs. shelled walnuts; grind in a grinder
2 cups sugar
1 and 1/2 cups milk
In a large sauce pan combine ground nuts and sugar.
Add warm milk to make a moist mixture cook
this over low-medium heat just until mixture
is warm; stir constantly.

TO MAKE ROLLS

Make small balls from the dough about the size of a walnut.

Roll the balls about 2 ½ inches in diameter in powdered sugar.
Put about 2 heaping teaspoons of filling in the
center of the dough.
Roll up and pinch dough together then roll again in
the powdered sugar; lots of powdered sugar again.
then shape into crescent rolls.

(You can make your balls into smaller circles if you prefer)

Place on greased baking sheet (or use parchment paper).
I like to use parchment paper.
It is best to place the pinched side of dough on the bottom when placing on cookie sheet

Brush rolls with beaten eggs. (about 2 eggs both whites and yolks)
Bake at 350° for 15 minutes or until golden brown.
Remove from cookie sheet cool on wire racks
Makes about 7 dozen rolls

Store in containers covered loosely with aluminum foil.
Do not store in air tight containers.

Wonderful gift at holiday time.

COLORING BOOK

Creative drawing was not a word that parents or teachers used in the 1950's. Drawing was seen as imitation or reproduction. The better I as a child was at imitating a picture that an artist had drawn, the better drawer I was considered to be. I still remember our blue drawing book. First, it showed the outline of a tree. The tree didn't have any branches. It was always in a full neat array of green leaves. However, the leaves were not individual leaves that fall to the ground or change color in the autumn, or even come to life in the spring. No, the leaves were all clumped together in a huge neat mass of green. There was never a mixture of greens or yellows or red. No the green color was the green color that you find in your basic box of eight Crayola crayons!

After I had mastered how to draw a tree, I was expected to add a house. Now this house was not really like any houses that were out in the farm country where I lived. No, this house that I drew belonged to some magic city where the houses were all neatly aligned exactly ten feet from the road, with a straight sidewalk, neatly bordered by flowers. No weeds in these flowerbeds! I felt I had to treat my colors carefully, peel back only enough of the paper so that the wax crayon was exposed. If I carefully rolled the crayon and used it from side to side I didn't have to sharpen it so often. Some children's crayons were like their desks, papers all shoved in helter-skelter, big books on top of smaller books, note books in sideways, spines going in either direction. What a mixed up mess. Maybe they were mixed up inside that way too!

One of my dad's favorite quotes was "cleanliness is next to godliness" and next in line was neatness. I don't remember questioning this design of a house, or whether that drawing was really art. This was what I was told to do, so this was what I did. So now, in my picture I would have a perfectly shaped tree, a neat house with a straight sidewalk bordered by flowers. For an added effect I sometimes added a cloud to the sky, with maybe the sun peeking out three fourths of the way! After the drawing was carefully drawn with a ruler, it could be colored.

Now, with such a neat drawing it was very important to color within the lines. Sloppy coloring ruined the picture! The drawing was graded by neatness, colors that matched, and straight lines. I as a child learned not to put orange next to red, only a light blue next to green, the sky was blue not purple, and if I put people in my pictures there was a crayon called flesh, a light pink! Maybe children in Africa were brown or black, but not in rural Wisconsin.

For another varied effect a bold move would be to color the flowers all different colors. I think maybe I knew instinctively as a child that the children who were the neat dressers were also the neat when coloring. None of this mixing plaid with prints!

An important step of moving up to second grade was to receive a bigger box of crayons, a box of sixteen crayons. When

I was finished using a color I put it back in its row. I remember children who seemed to think they could get a new box of crayons by snapping their fingers and within three or four weeks of school starting had most of their crayons broken. I knew my box had to last the whole year, so I better be careful. I usually only loaned them out to a desperate kid who needed a crayon to finish his drawing assignment on time.

The tough color to keep was red. It was the brightest. It was the prettiest. It always wore down first. I never knew why the crayon people didn't put two red crayons in the box and leave out white. Where did I need to use white? The art paper was white, so just leave it blank!

Art as it was called was always due on Fridays before the last recess, 2:15 to 2:30 PM.

The students in the primary grades could bring a coloring book to school. This could be used when your schoolwork was all finished.

I loved to color. I loved to be careful and stay in the lines. I knew how to be neat. I got all upset when several of my friends colored in my coloring books and didn't stay within the line. How sloppy. My mother bought me a new coloring book after one had become ruined. She paid 39 cents for it. I made her write on the outside cover "Louise is the only person allowed to color in this book." I wanted a perfect coloring book. I wanted neat pictures. I didn't want any pictures going outside the lines. I figured if I was the only one to color in it, I could have it perfect.

I wanted a perfect book. I wanted all the pictures well executed. I wanted all the colors matching. I wanted my new coloring book all neat and tidy. It should look like an art book. I wanted my dad to be proud of me. A couple of my best friends were the sloppiest when coloring. They didn't know how to stay in the line or how to have two colors meet neatly next to each other, but not bump. I knew how to press hard on the crayon, but not streak the wax crayon. I wanted only Cathy to color in my book. She was the best.

The coloring book was perhaps seen as a reflection on a child's dress habits or housekeeping skills. It was really very important. Ironic though, Kathy's desk was always messy and she never could find a thing in it yet she was one of the best artists in school.

Later on, when I reached 6th grade, I received a box of 48 crayons. I was so excited. Wow! Super! Incredible! This was spectacular!

The rainbows, the flowers, and the buildings I could draw with my new box of crayons. But alas, I could not create pictures. I copied other artist's drawings. I sometimes drew my own house, or the school building or church, but I don't remember doing the cemetery, or a tree with branches or a variety of flowers. I usually drew tulips. These I could draw nice and even.

Another favorite picture I liked to draw was the cross of Jesus. Jesus would be in the center of the picture and one cross on each side. This is the scene of the crucifixion, with the two criminals that were also meeting their death that day. The King James Bible calls them malefactors. The words Jesus spoke on the cross would be put in the clouds. Never do I remember a figure being drawn on the cross, only the sign that Pilate posted on the cross, "Jesus Christ, King of the Jews." The disciples were nowhere to be seen. I guess they all fled.

Some children were really sloppy at drawing. They just wanted to get a picture done and didn't care if they wasted their coloring book, crayons or time. A few children in the school were super drawers though. They made pictures up that looked like an artist. Cathy, the chatterbox, could draw anything and make it look real. And it didn't take her long either. She saw pictures in her head. She didn't need the drawing book. After Cathy graduated, Lee became the school artist. He too could see pictures in his head and make them look real. Today he works in an art museum, so I guess he's still seeing pictures in his head. I'm not sure how Cathy and Lee saw pictures in their head, but I feel some of it is because as children they didn't feel the same rules as fiercely as I did. I think some children are naturally more talented and see the world through different eyes. I needed to be praised by my dad, the teacher. I needed to draw the only way that I knew to please him.

Most of us children needed the drawing book to see pictures. They weren't quite real, but then we had not seen Picasso or Klee or heard of O'Keefe. Art museums or paintings were in a world unknown to rural Wisconsin farm children, so coloring books were the only art we knew.

Looking back, it's hard to believe. Creativity, imagination, exploration became popular concepts of the sixties. Maybe modern art teachers in the big cities of Chicago and Milwaukee, helped their students see pictures in their head, but art, like religion was a narrow world in rural Wisconsin.

Rules were drawn like staying within the lines. I learned not to question. How is it that Cathy could see pictures in her head and I could only copy? Maybe she had a freedom to see. Why I ask myself didn't I question? Maybe it was because after all, I was only a child.

HEAVENLY BARS

2 cups raisins (or 1 cup raisins and 1 cup chopped dates)
1/2 cup brown sugar
1 1/2 cup water
Boil together until done.
Add 1 teaspoon vanilla and 1 Tablespoon flour, mixed with water.
Boil until thick.

Set aside.

Mix in bowl:
1 cup flour
1 tsp. baking soda
1 cup brown sugar
3/4 cup melted shortening
2 cups rolled oaks

Pat about 3/4 of this mixture in a pan about 9" x 12" in size.
Add filling and sprinkle rest of mixture over it.
Bake 25 minutes in 350-degree
Optional: sprinkle coconut or nut meats on top.

Alternate filling is 1 can cheery pie filling or other thickened fruit.

All-time family favorite.

THE PIANO LESSON

Plink! Plink! Plink! Plink! Plink! Bong! Oops, I was another student trying to play a tune. It's a long road from piano lessons in the back living room of rural Wisconsin to the Carnegie concert Hall in New York City. Piano lessons permeated our house as my mother tried to give rural youngsters a chance at playing an instrument and instilling in them a sense of music appreciation. She gave piano lessons over every lunch hour, every day after school and most evenings, day after day after day.

My mother had learned to play the piano very well growing up on a prosperous farm outside of Green Bay, Wisconsin. She had lessons over eight years. By giving lessons to the children in the countryside where my dad was a school teacher, she not only helped these children learn music, but also helped earn some extra money for her family. A country parochial school teacher did not make enough money to give his family any extra conveniences.

My mother was able to teach her students theory as well as simply playing a tune. She would teach them the meaning of whole notes, the round hollow notes, with no stems. The students learned that whole notes got four beats: 1, 2, 3, 4 would be tapped out. A whole rest would be counted, 1, 2, 3, 4 before you continue to play. Then a student learned about half notes, a hollow note, but with a stem. This was counted as 1, 2. Two half notes equal one whole note. My mother then showed them the equation one whole note equals two halves. Now on to quarter notes. She would explain that they were just like four quarters in a dollar bill, "Four quarter notes equal one whole note, 1, 2, 3, 4. Now to play, 1, 2, 3, 4, or 1 and, 2 and, 3 and, 4 and, or more evenly 1, 2, 3, 4. I think you have it. Let's do it again, and again, and again. Now for the left hand and here we go again."

If the student caught on, my mother might attempt to explain ¾ rhythm and the difference between it and 4/4 time or rhythm as she called it. Sometime later down the road the two hands would be joined to play at the same time. This was a big step indeed and didn't usually come for at least two or three months after the student started taking lessons.

Plink, plink, plink, and plunk, over and over again. Then she would move on to teach the scales. First the C Major scale was taught as it has no sharps or flats. And what is a sharp? What is a flat? It is not the same as singing sharp or flat. Probably the idea was taken from that sense of singing a bit higher than being on tune, or a bit flatter than being off tune. A sharp is a half step or tone higher, thus usually the black key to the right of the white key for which it is named, or the black key to the white keys left for the flat.

And now the half hour is over, and the next student is waiting her turn. Mainly my mother's students were children from the grade school where my dad taught, but a few students were from the neighboring towns. These were the after supper lessons.

Every day when I came home from school, I had to peel potatoes, or clean carrots, wash the lettuce, set the table, and fry the meat because my mother would be busy giving piano lessons. I could peel to the plinking of the piano, or the 1, 2, 3, 4, count of the metronome. The metronome was the little wind-up machine that kept perfect rhythm and to which a student was to attempt to imitate. Like trying to thread a needle at first it seemed an almost impossible task.

In the kitchen, my brother and I were expected to be quiet. We were not to disturb the lesson. We dared not question about the students taking away our free time. My mother was getting paid for giving lessons, and we were to be thankful that she had so many students.

We too had to take lessons also, like it or not. Well, I liked playing the piano. I still do. I hated the repetitive exercises. I disliked the metronome and having to count all the notes carefully in correct rhythm. I just wanted to play the tunes that I knew. I didn't want to play the old masters from the past. In sixth grade my mother gave me the sheet music to "White Christmas." It was wonderful even though I suspected that the introduction contained a scale, and the rhythm looked very similar to the 4/4 rhythm of an exercise that I had. It was music I recognized. I loved the words. I could pretend I was singing along with Bing Crosby. I pretended I was on the radio, making it into the big-time.

By the end of that winter I am sure my family was very happy to hear the end of "White Christmas" and get into a new phase as my mother called my attraction to the different singers. It wasn't long before Elvis appeared on the scene. I purchased the sheet music to "Love me tender" and "Jailhouse Rock." I was not allowed to buy records as my parents saw them as a waste of money, but I could buy sheet music. I'm sure my mother figured that maybe if I learned to enjoy playing the piano and she suffered through my pop music, someday I would switch to, and begin to appreciate Beethoven, Bach and all those other old men as I considered them. And she was right!

In the meantime, while my mother was giving piano lessons I was to make dinner, with NO NOISE. My dad was usually in his study, recuperating from the day's teaching, or running a few errands before dinner.

Sometimes my mother had made desert, like apple cobbler (fresh apples peeled, cooked with cinnamon sugar and a little flour to thicken, topped with a pastry crust, none better) or perhaps fresh home-made donuts, all lined up on the bread board like wheels on a car. If she hadn't put some in the freezer, they would be all eaten before the end of the lessons. It was very easy to eat three or four. The soft fresh dough, topped with powdered sugar just melted in my mouth. I was in my twenties, before I realized that some mothers never baked donuts, and actually bought them from a bakery shop. These though could never have been as good as homemade.

After the last afternoon lesson, it was time for dinner. If the timing went well, everyone was home: my sister from high school, the oldest sister from her secretarial job in the city, and my oldest brother home from the paper mill. Unless he was working the three to eleven shifts, there were seven in all at the dinner table.

We each had our assigned place to sit. My dad sat at the head of the table. My mother sat at the other end. My youngest brother sat next to my mother. I had to sit next to my dad then came my oldest sister. On the other side of the table was the next oldest sister and my oldest brother. Milk was poured for each of us children, which was all except LeAnne. She refused to drink milk. This was almost unheard of in the country, but ironically she has the best teeth of us all. My mother and dad drank instant coffee.

I'm not sure why my mother didn't perk coffee. Maybe she didn't have a percolator. My parents always drank instant coffee, and I did too until well into my twenties.

Prayers were said. It was always the same prayer before dinner, "Come Lord Jesus be our guest and let these gifts to us be blest." I don't ever remember a variation on the opening prayer. Nothing personal was ever added or suggested. This was the old family German method.

After the opening prayer, everyone spoke of the day's activities. Sometimes it seemed we all talked at once, or whoever could get started first or who was the loudest! Depending on the evening schedules, dinner would last from twenty minutes to an hour. It was a fun sharing time. After we were done eating, the meal was finished with a Bible reading, devotion and prayer.

Then we each had our assigned chores: clear the table, put the food away, wash the dishes, dry the dishes, and put them away. Usually before this was all done, another piano student had arrived and my mother would whisk her away to the back room. We were given our usual reminder to keep the noise down. My mother had both boys and girls for lessons, but most of the farm boys had chores so there were fewer boys taking lessons after school and in the evenings.

After dishes it was time for my brother and me to do our homework. Sometimes if we were lucky we would get to watch a television show. That is, if we kept the volume down. Sometimes I visited with the mothers who came in the evening bringing their child.

I remember Mrs. Lehman. She usually brought some paperwork as her and her husband ran a small cheese factory in the neighboring town. But she always asked me about school, how things were going and generally just made me feel important. Some mothers brought handwork or mending along. No one just sat, but most of them stayed and sat around our kitchen table, rather than drive back and forth to their home. That would have been considered wasting gas and time.

The lessons were usually finished by 8:30 or 9 P.M. That's usually when we got to watch television if the homework was finished. "I love Lucy," "December Bride," "I've got a Secret," were some of the favorite shows in those days. The set actually belonged to my oldest brother, but it was set in the living room and we'd all watch it together. Since he was out working at the mill, he bought the set for the whole family to enjoy.

How did the students fare? Well, some of the students went on to play in the high school band, others sang in the high school chorus, for now they could read music, and several students became the accompanist for the high school chorus. Another student became the church organist after my parents moved to another town. All the years at this country parish my dad was the organist, and sometimes I accompanied the choir on the organ so that he could stand and direct the choir.

Plink, plink, plink, plink, many things have small beginnings. Giving the young people from this rural area a chance to appreciate music was perhaps my mother's greatest gift to this country community.

EIGHT LAYER CASSEROLE

1 lb. ground beef
1 onion chopped
3 Tablespoons rice
1 can condensed tomato soup
3 carrots sliced
1 cup diced celery
1 green pepper chopped
2 potatoes sliced

Brown beef, add onion and rice.
Simmer for 5 – 10 minutes.
Place meat mixture at the bottom of a 3 quart casserole dish.
Layer carrots, celery, green pepper, potatoes in casserole.
Pour tomato soup, (diluted with can of water) over mixture.
Cover and bake for 1 ½ hours.
Salt to taste.
Makes 4 – 5 servings.

Tasty winter dinner.

ROSES... WAXED ROSES

Pink, yellow, white and red, but red roses never turned out as well. My mother even made a few blue ones. But blue roses never were popular.

My mother started making paper flowers when she was a young girl. She had a pattern book and just started cutting out patterns. Soon she could make just about any kind of flower out of paper. She discovered that crepe paper worked best. She could twist it and turn it and roll it around a knitting needle. Sometime she put several colors together. She cut out all different shapes and could make irises, carnations and gladiolas. Her favorite flower to make was the rose.

The crepe paper is cut, folded and then twisted around a piece of wire. She started experimenting with paraffin. She dipped the crepe paper flower into hot wax, again, and again. My mother dipped the flower seven times in all, letting the wax dry each time. She also made a bud to match the color of the rose and then added a few leaves. All were twisted together on the wire stem.

Sometimes when I came home from school and my mother was busy waxing the flowers I would dip my fingers in the hot wax. It wasn't boiling so I didn't burn myself. As soon as I took my hand out the wax would harden. Very carefully I would start moving my fingers and gently pull them out of the wax form. Then I had my hand in an impression. Being hollow my wax fingers soon broke. Then I would put the wax back in the pan with the other wax that needed to be melted again on the stove.

The small table fan quickly dries the wax between layers. Florist tape is wrapped around the wire. Then the wire is bent so that the rose laid on the table looks like a natural creation. It was a beautiful waxed rose. After all the layers of wax, I couldn't tell there was crepe paper underneath the wax. They seemed unreal. The roses are carefully wrapped in cellophane and packed in a big box, six to eight roses in a box.

Then my work begins. My dad drives me to the nearest big town and lets me off on a street corner with rather nice looking houses. We agree to meet in two hours at the same spot. He will do some shopping. He will probably go to a garage and find a mechanic to talk to. My dad can talk to anyone on any subject for hours on end. It stimulates him and he never tires of it, but it drives my mother crazy.

Here I am at my first house. It was always hard to get started. I had to give myself a pep talk that I could do this. I had to tell myself that people would like me and like my product and buy a rose.

I was about twelve at the time when I first started selling roses. I would ring the doorbell and say, "Hello, I'm Louise. I'd like to show you these waxed roses that I'm selling for my Mother. They're only seventy-five cents each. They come in red, pink, and yellow. Some people buy three and put a candle in the middle."

Sometimes a woman would ask if the flowers could be washed. "Yes, they're washable or you can just gently wipe off the dust. "Would you like one?"

If the woman said, "Yes, please," I would break out in a smile and say, "Thank you very much. My mother's name is on this tag if you'd like to order another one sometime. Thank you. Good-bye."

One sold, I only had seven more to sell. My mother would give me a quarter for each rose that I sold. I really wanted to make two dollars, but that seemed a very high goal.

When I came to a house and the woman wasn't home it was always a disappointment, "Oh, your wife's not home. The flower makes a nice present."

Sometimes the man would say, "She just had her birthday?"

Then I'd suggest, "How about one for your sister or an aunt?"

"No, he didn't think so."

"I see. Well, thank you anyway. Maybe another time. Good-bye."

A husband hardly ever bought a flower if his wife wasn't at home. Then I would have to get my courage all built up again to go to the next house to sell. I gave myself another pep talk.

"Well, try another house, Louise. You're sure to get another sale."

Knock, knock.

"I'd like to show you this beautiful waxed rose made by my mother. They make lovely gifts. They cost only seventy-five cents. I'm from the country, near Fremont."

If she seemed a bit interested, I might add, "Oh, she's been making them for years. Would you like to see a yellow one?"

Perhaps now, the lady invited me inside the house. Then I'd take out several different colors and elaborate.

"Well, some people mix the colors. Yellow, white and pink go very nicely together."

If I made a sale, I might close with saying, "I hope you'll like it. Thank you very much."

Good, two sold, and it's only 2:30. One-and-a-half hours to go. I've made fifty cents. Oh, how I'd love to sell all eight. $2.00. If I add it to the money I made with babysitting I should have enough to buy a new blouse. Or maybe my Mother would let me buy some new material for a new spring dress.

Oh, there's my Dad.

"Yes Dad, I sold five. I guess that was not so bad. I even met a lady who was also a teacher and she knew Pastor Simon. Well, yes I'm ready to quit."

"Maybe next week I can sell more. It'll be closer to Easter. Flowers make a nice spring gift."

DILL PICKLES WITH GARLIC

Place whole medium sized cucumbers in quart jars

Mix following ingredients in 3 quart pan:
1 1/2 cup vinegar
1/2 cup salt
2 quarts water
Slice of onion
Size of pea of alum
If desired: clove of garlic
Dill
Let come to a boil and pour over pickles in jars and seal.

For those who like a tinge of garlic.

CANNING PROCCESS

After cucumbers, or other food, is put in the canning jars with its brine, or other liquid, wipe threads and top of jar with warm clean cloth. Put on new lids and covers and screw tight. Place jars in canner, e.g. large kettle with wire rack that holds 6 jars. Cover jars with water. Bring water to boil and boil 20 minutes. Raise wire rack and let jars cool off gradually. As jars cool, a popping sound will indicate a secure seal. When water reaches room temperature, jars can be removed from canner. Place jars on a towel and check jars if sealed. Middle of lid will be indented. This can take up to 24 hours. Store in a cool dry space up to 12 months.

PICKING PICKLES

STOP, BEND, PICK, PING, LIFT BUCKET, AND WALK ON. STOP, BEND, PICK, PING, LIFT BUCKET, AND WALK ON. STOP, BEND, PICK, PING, LIFT BUCKET, AND WALK ON...

It was mid-July in Wisconsin. It was hot and humid. There would probably be a thundershower by evening. The cucumbers that had been so carefully planted Memorial weekend were now shining forth and needed picking. If the cucumbers didn't get picked every day in this hot and humid weather they would grow much too large. Large cucumbers were nice for home canning, but not to take in to the Squire Dingee Pickle Factory. The smaller the better. The cucumbers got graded for size, and the smaller number one size cucumbers were worth lots more money than the oversized number fives. Even so, you always missed a few and ended up with a bucket of oversized cucumbers. These big clunkers my mother would pickle for home use, slice up for salad, or chop up for relish. None really went to waste, but the idea was for the pickle patch to make money.

We wanted a new television set. My older brother had bought the first one and he was getting married this summer. Well, the TV was his so he would be taking it to his new home. So we needed to buy a new one for our house. So, picking pickles was the way to get the new television.

After an hour or so of bending over, my back ached. I was sweaty and smelly. The cows next door didn't help; they attracted the flies. I wore rubber gloves to keep my fingers clean. They were filled with talcum power so you could slip them off after you got all sticky.

Picking pickles wasn't much fun.

When my bucket was full, I had to carry it to the bottom of the row and pour them into a gunnysack. A gunny sack is just another name for a burlap bag. Some people used feed bags, but gunny sacks were better, as there really was no other use for them. A feed bag, usually, was sturdy cotton, and my mother would sew dresses from them for me and my sisters. Feed bags were usually were decorated with flowers or geometric designs and they seem to wear forever, or until I outgrew them.

If it was a good day's picking, I would get four or five bags of cucumbers. This would take the whole morning and sometimes the whole afternoon. Then they were loaded into the trunk of the car and my dad, brother and I would be off to the Squire Dingee Pickle Factory.

My sisters were lucky. The oldest one was married already, so that let her off the hook, and the other one was old enough to get a job away from home. And what was her job? She was the bookkeeper at the Squire Dingee Pickle Factory. She just had to sit behind a window, taking in the sheets of tallies which showed how many pounds of what size cucumbers people brought in. She figured out how much they were owed, and wrote out the check.

At the pickle factory the cucumbers were loaded on a conveyer belt. This went up an incline where there were graders and sorted the cucumbers out by size. They fell into different buckets. Each bucket was weighed by the pickle manager and he wrote this down on a slip of paper. This paper was then given to my sister to do her figuring.

The pickles then were put in huge vats of brine. It was fun to walk around and see all the pickles floating in the brine. What a smell? After a few weeks, or sometimes months, the pickles were shipped out by train to the company's canning factory in Chicago.

I thought my sister had an easy job compared to mine. What a job. I had to pick these silly green things. My little brother helped, but being five years younger… he naturally wasn't as good as me. My mother helped sometimes, if she didn't have the laundry, or a piano lesson, or something else to do, but I wanted a television, so pick pickles I did.

If we had a good summer, we might make more than just for the television. The extra money would go for a vacation fund, school clothes, and next year's garden supplies. Even though my parents got a free house, as my dad worked for the church, raising five children wasn't easy on a church salary.

Besides the cucumbers to pick, we had a full vegetable garden. I remember that my dad especially liked to grow corn and potatoes. For some reason, maybe just to relax, my dad often went out to the garden after church. Mother would get very angry if he went out in his Sunday clothes. Somehow, it seemed to me as a child they often did things just to aggravate each other.

The thing I didn't like about the cornfield was the fungus that grew on some of them. It was scary. It would be all puffy and then turn black. But fresh corn from the garden was stupendous. Potato digging was not too awfully bad; I had to use a pitchfork and hopefully as I dug down I didn't split a potato. I was just supposed to loosen the dirt a bit and then pull the plant up and hopefully there were potatoes hanging on the end. The bucket got filled a lot quicker with potatoes than with cucumbers!

Tomatoes, beets, carrots, spinach, lettuce, kohlrabi, rhubarb, these all grew in abundance in our garden. All summer long my family feasted on fresh vegetables. My mother was kept busy canning so that we could enjoy them all winter long.

My parents bought a chest freezer with the pickle money. First we had a fairly small one, nine cubic feet. Then they traded it in for one that was double in size. It took over one whole kitchen wall. It had two doors. It was very convenient to put stuff on and we were constantly shuffling books back and forth between the two doors.

Besides the food from the garden we would get some fruit from the neighbors. We didn't have any apple trees, but several neighbors did and we could come and get as much as we needed. Another neighbor had currants. My mother would make jelly. She would usually buy some raspberries from the nursery and we would make a trip up to Door county to pick cherries.

Picking cherries was another high adventure. The trees would be brimming with cherries. Large wooden ladders would be next to a tree. I took my bucket and climbed up as far as I dared and started picking. Of course the fun thing was, I could eat as many as I wanted too, and these were free.

How could they charge me for cherries in my tummy? My family usually picked around 100 pounds. I remember that they cost about ten cents a pound. After we got the cherries home, they had to be pitted, one by one, cherry by cherry. Thumbnails worked the best. Wearing gloves was impossible. By the end of picking out the pits, my thumbs had changed to a lovely red hue that lasted for over a week. But I would be thinking of all the cherry pies, and cobblers that this enabled my mom to make.

We also grew dill. With dill, mother could make all the dill pickles we could eat for a year. I did pick enough pickles that summer to get a new 17 inch black and white Zenith television. Life was good.

DILL PICKLES

Pack the cucumbers in a pint or quart canning jar.

Boil all together:
2 quarts water
1 quart vinegar
1 cup salt

Add:
1 scant teaspoon powdered alum
2 stalks of dill per quart.

Pour vinegar mixture over pickles while hot
Screw lids on tightly.
Cover.
Jars will give a popping sound when sealed.

Most summers my mom canned over 100 quarts of dill pickles.

BERRY BERRY QUITE CONTRARY

Out in the country there were not many opportunities for a young girl to make money. The usual way after about the age of twelve was babysitting. Young families in the neighborhood would sometimes go into the city for a movie, or a wedding dance and not want to be bothered with their children. This however, was not a steady income, as most young farm families, did not go out on a regular basis.

I enjoyed babysitting. It gave me a chance to see how the other people lived. I played with the children until their bedtime. As I saw it, I then got paid for reading, doing homework, or watching television until the parents came home.

However, my main source of income in the years between ten and sixteen was berry picking. Two miles from our home was the village of Readfield. A family comprised of an elderly couple, and her older brother had acres and acres of land turned into a nursery. It was filled with strawberry, raspberry, and blackberry fields. They had many different varieties, and the raspberry bushes and strawberry plants were lined up row after row after row.

My sister next in age to me got the job before me to help pick berries. One of the men would drive out to the country homes and pick up a number of young girls and boys to help them harvest their crop. As berries usually got ripe all about the same time, it was important to get them picked the morning that they were at their prime.

The summer when I had turned ten I was told I was old enough to start if I did a good job. I was very excited about doing this. I already had been picking cucumbers for a number of years. I knew it was hard work. But out in the nursery, I would be with a bunch of other children my age, and get to keep the money I earned.

I would be picked up around seven in the morning, except at the height of the raspberry season it was often as early as six o'clock. The air was quite cool at that time of day. I would have to dress in layers. I would have my shorts and halter top on, but over it would be an old shirt, maybe a pair of pants, and an old jacket. Then after working awhile, and the sun went higher and higher in the sky, the layers of clothing would come off.

Sometimes, the manager would bring us children out something to drink in the fields, but usually we just endured the heat. We could eat all the berries that we wanted. The only trouble with that was that it would keep our boxes from filling up. For raspberry picking we wore a box around our waist that held two one-quart boxes. I stood in front of a bush, and dropped the berries in one by one. As I got better at it, I picked with both hands, filled my right hand up and then dropped the berries into the box, not stopping while continuing to pick with my left hand. All the while my eyes were looking for where they were more berries on the bush. Berries hid under the leaves and some berries were close to the ground. The owners were very unhappy if I or any of their pickers kept ripe berries on a bush.

They would be overripe for the next picking and thus a loss. I also knew that Mandie, the bosses' wife, would remove any berries that were not ripe out of our box. She was very particular.

After I had picked my two boxes full, I would have to carry it to the end of the row. There I would have placed a container that held eight quarts. When this was full, I had to carry it to the barn for it to be credited to my account. The owners expected you to heap your boxes, so that it was a good full quart. Sometimes I over heaped them, and then I could get credit for nine or even ten quarts. But I had to be careful. If I heaped the box too much Mandie could be upset that I was smashing the berries.

It wasn't long before I was known to be one of the best pickers. I was happy picking berries. It was a way to earn some extra money. How much money did I earn? All the other pickers, and I received seven cents a quart for raspberries, and five cents a quart for strawberries. Strawberries generally are bigger than raspberries, so I guess they figured strawberries could fill up the containers faster. They didn't have as many strawberries fields though and it was harder work.

In strawberry picking I had to take my eight-pack container with me down the row as I crawled along inch by inch. It was a backbreaking job. They started growing some of the bigger varieties of bigger berries, but the smaller jam berry was the favorite of most of their customers. No matter the size, the wage was five cents a quart.

Mandie would keep track of each container that I brought in. It was written on straps of old quart boxes in her scrawny handwriting. She recorded it in her book, and at the end of the day I took my strap of wood home. I kept these in a cup on my shelf. As it was, Mandie and Ollie did not pay their workers until the end of the season. I am not sure why this is. I don't think that would be allowed today.

All of us young pickers were expected to pick the whole season, which was usually mid-June until early August. I got paid at the end of the strawberry season and then again at the end of the raspberry season. There weren't that many blackberries and they were counted in with the raspberries.

In a good day of picking strawberries I could pick forty quarts. That is a lot of berries. I earned two dollars. It is hard to put it in perspective with today's wages, as back then candy bars were still a nickel, a double-dip ice cream cone cost a dime, a nice white blouse cost five dollars and a pair of sturdy black and white saddle shoes could be bought for ten dollars.

At the end of the strawberry season I usually made around thirty-five dollars. It was not a lot of money, but more than I could make babysitting. It was a good job for a country girl. I didn't live on a farm so I didn't have the usual farm chores like milking cows and hauling in hay that many of the farm children were expected to do.

In raspberries I did even better as I made seven cents a quart. Often in the peak of the season I could pick eighty-five to a hundred quarts a day. The peak season only lasted a week or ten days, but those were glorious days. When I made seven dollars a day, I felt glorious. On those peak days, I would be picking morning and afternoon.

Hank, Mandie's brother, would drive us home for lunch and then come back in about an hour to pick us up for the afternoon picking. By then it would be quite hot, and sometimes we could talk Hank into stopping at the bar to buy us a Popsicle or maybe an ice cream drumstick and if he was in a really good mood also a soda pop.

Hank had a little dog that he really loved. It was a little Mexican Chihuahua. He climbed all over the car and usually got into some kind of trouble. Hank loved to stop at the local bar and buy himself a drink. I think we all knew that Hank drank beer and even whiskey at times. His breath was awful. But Hank loved his little Chihuahua. He was good at heart. He would usually get all of us children an ice cream or soda treat from the bar when he stopped. Sometimes, I knew he had too much to drink and didn't handle his station wagon very well. I would have to tell him where to turn, and remind him that a car was coming.

This was before the days of seat belts. These were country roads and generally not too much traffic, but it would be no fun to land in the ditch. He loved to tease us children, and generally the ride home was fun.

Hank loved to go fishing and would keep his catches in a copper tank near the berry barn. He loved to show off his big catfish and tease us with them. I thought they were ugly. Even though Hank would offer them to us to take home, I never could see myself eating them, so I never took any home with me.

In the peak of the season they asked me to pick on Sundays. I had to go to church in the morning, but my parents allowed me to pick in the afternoon. I would be paid ten cents a quart. Again, Hank or Ollie came and drove me and the few others who were able to pick on Sundays. We were usually treated to ice cream bars or some special treat, as Hank was happy that we were helping him out. This was usually quite easy to do.

Sometimes Ollie, Mandie's husband drove us home. Ollie didn't usually stop at the bar. He was more serious. But, he drove the pick-up truck, and so all of us berry pickers would ride in the back of the truck. We would be happy that the days work was done. We would sing songs and tell jokes.

When Ollie came to our house he would come to a quick stop and we'd jump off the back. Ollie would holler, "See you tomorrow. Be ready at six A.M." And the truck continued down the country road. It was time for a bath and a good scrub. Although sometimes, I then had to help my mother and brother finish picking pickles before I could get cleaned up.

The other aspect of berry picking was the fun times in the fields with all the other children. It was a time for telling jokes, singing songs and making up stories. Sometimes while raspberry picking, I usually picked with a partner so that each side of the bush could be covered, I would get into a heavy discussion about movie stars, country living, God, church, and other concerns that most young people have today.

One time as I was picking raspberries I put my hand in the bush and much to my surprise I had put my hand into a bee's nest. Ouch. I let out a loud scream. I was wearing shorts and my halter-top. The bees attacked my stomach area. They were everywhere. One of the other pickers hollered for Mandie and Ollie. Quickly, a paste of mud was made and smeared all over my bee stings. I had something like twenty-five stings. Oh, it hurt. The hurt of the stings made my eyes water.

The mud miraculously helped take out the sting. There were swollen marks where the sting had gone in, but I was okay. When I came home, my mother made a paste of baking soda. Fortunately, I wasn't allergic to bee stings, but I can still feel the sensation of all those bees swarming around me.

Another time going down the row, I saw a big snake. I knew most snakes in Wisconsin were harmless and yet I sure didn't like them. I hollered out for the others to come see. He was really a fat snake. He was slithering slowly along. We decided we should try and kill him. We found some stones lying around the berry patch and proceeded to throw them at him. He soon was dead.

We were all curious why he was so fat. We decided to investigate. He was dead anyway. One of the boys had a jackknife. He proceeded to cut open the snake. And much to our surprise there was a frog lodged in the upper area where the big bulge was. While stunned, it took the frog only a moment or two, to realize his freedom was at hand, and he hopped out of the snake. By then, Ollie was on the scene and came to see what the excitement was all about. With a big shovel, Ollie scooped up the snake and took him away. "Back to work children," said Ollie. And so on with berry picking we went.

One hot summer day we thought it would be fun to pretend that we were all DJs on a local radio show. We all took different parts. We made up call letters for our station. We decided on WBER. I became the news broadcaster and gave a quick headline of all the local news events. This could include events about President Eisenhower, as well as news, of what the local farmers were growing in their fields. Another berry picker was the sports broadcaster and told about the Braves and also the local softball teams. And, another berry picker gave the weather forecast. A few of the pickers were the music team, and they sang the songs of the day. Many times, we all joined in and made up verses as we went along.

There were also favorite local songs, like "The Old Beer Bottle":

The old beer bottle, drifting helplessly.
The old beer bottle, a thousand miles from home.
The old beer bottle just floating down the foam.
And in it was a message, these words were written on,
"Whoever finds this bottle will find the beer all gone."
I'm like this empty bottle, drifting helplessly;
Without a heart since we're apart, there's nothing left.
The old beer bottle, floating down the foam, etc.
(Origin unknown).

The day wouldn't be complete without singing "One Hundred Bottles of Beer in the Wall":

> One hundred bottles of beer in the wall,
> One hundred bottles of beer.
> Take one down and pass it around,
> 99 bottles of beer in the wall.
> Ninety-nine bottles of beer in the wall,
> 99 bottles of beer,
> Take one down and pass it around,
> 98 bottles of beer in the wall, etc.
> (Origin unknown).

We faithfully would sing all one hundred verses.

It was a good way to help pass the day. It made us forgot how hot we were getting, or the bug bites or thinking about children in the city who were at the swimming pool just lying around. It made us feel part of a team, and that we weren't just bumpkin country kids.

As I got older picking berries and was already in high school, it became the place where I planned my evening activities. Maybe, somebody could get the family car and I could go along to see a movie.

Sometimes, there was a DJ dance in New London, and I could plan to drive in with them. Rather than being isolated out in the country, berry picking brought me closer to the other country children and we became a team. It helped me meet other children who went to the local public schools that often had different religious backgrounds. It opened my world a bit further as I was beginning to make new friends and not just be the teacher's kid.

I still have a great fondness for any kind of berry. And actually I never have had the courage to eat catfish. I remember how ugly they always looked in Hank's big tank behind the barn.

EASY SUMMER SALAD

Bowl of fresh cut leaf lettuce.
Clean.
Sprinkle 1 Tablespoon sugar over lettuce.
Squeeze juice of one orange over lettuce.
Mix
If desired, cut up second orange in bite size pieces and mix with lettuce.

Serve immediately.

Great on a hot summer day.

SEEING THE USA

Where does a family go on vacation with five children? That was before the Holiday Inn, Ramada Inn, or even Motel 6. There was no Triple A guidebook to give you a trip-tick!

Taking five children on vacation is certainly an adventure. Looking back now I am amazed that my parents even considered going on any trips considering the cost. My dad especially loved to travel.

Working for a church school and being the church organist certainly limited the time that we could be gone. It had to be after church on Sunday, and back before the following Sunday service. But then we didn't have any cows to milk or pigs to feed, so I guess the farmers didn't think being back for Sunday services was such a hardship.

But we certainly didn't travel first class. We had a 1946 Chevy. It was a 4-door two-toned green sedan. There were no seat belts. It had no turn signals. The car had no defrost system.

Where did we all sit? My baby brother and I were on laps. The three older children sat in the back seat. Food would be packed for lunch and supper. This was before McDonald's and other fast food restaurants. I was in high school before I remember my parents ever eating out in a restaurant.

The first family vacation that I remember was a trip to Duluth, Minnesota. It was to see the big pit made by the copper mines. From Duluth we would go on to visit some cousins in Minnesota that my dad wanted to get in touch with. I remember it was getting dark. We were all getting tired. Where were we going to sleep that night? It seemed confusing and I was getting worried. Nobody tells a five-year-old anything.

The road was dark. And we just kept driving and driving. We stopped. The sign said NO VACANCY. No room. The place had no rooms or cabins left. We drove on. And then there was a light in the distance. We could see some cabins back near some trees. The sign said VACANCY. That was good.

Daddy went in. We waited in the car. We could stay there, but it would be crowded. The man had only two beds in one small cabin. We would stay. We had been driving all day. Everyone was tired. We piled out of the car. There was a screen door on the cabin. A flycatcher hung from the outside light bulb.

We all filed into the cabin. The room had a linoleum floor. There was just one overhead light. There was no indoor plumbing. We had to use the outside bathroom. There was an indoor sink in the room. It had a pump with a handle to pump water. To get hot water we had to heat it on the cook stove that was in the corner. That was the only heat for the room. It had one double bed and a rollaway. There were seven of us. My mother decided that if we five children lay across the bed we would all fit. But it seemed so scary. I don't remember where my baby brother slept. He probably slept between us. This was not like home. Where were we?

The light went out. Sounds of the highway could be heard. What if someone came to the door?

"Sh… Louise. Go to sleep," my older sister said.

"I'm scared."

"Say your prayers," my mother interjected.

I had a whole set of prayers. My two favorites were: "Now I lay me down to sleep, I pray the Lord my soul to keep; if I should die before I wake, I pray the Lord my soul to take; and this I ask for Jesus' sake"; followed by "Jesus tender, Shepherd, hear me; bless Thy little lamb tonight; though the darkness be Thou near me; Keep me safe till morning light."

And overcome by exhaustion, I fell asleep.

After touring Duluth the next day, we drove on to my cousins in Minnesota who lived on a farm.

Now these cousins seemed strange. They wore old-fashioned clothes. The men wore suspenders. They lived in a big old farmhouse with big cupboards and a big pump by the kitchen sink.

I didn't know anybody. I don't remember seeing them before. My older brother and two older sisters went down to a neighboring cousin's farm, while my baby brother and I stayed with my parents with these old folks.

My brother and sisters came by riding on ponies. That looked like fun. I got to ride with my brother. I felt so big. Even my baby brother got put on a pony. Then I got to ride all by myself. This was fun. I wanted to ride all day.

Then more cousins came over. There were so many of them. We all got lined up to have our picture taken. I was the only little girl. I liked visiting my cousins in Wisconsin a whole lot better. In Wisconsin there were a lot of children and the farmers didn't wear suspenders.

These were all old looking farmers. How did we know them anyway? To this day, I don't know, but I remember my dad writing to them and talking about our cousins in Minnesota.

We also had cousins who lived near Niagara Falls. A trip was planned there when I was about ten years old. We had new 1954 Chevrolet. It was a pretty lime green car.

We were to stay in a motel along the way. This time it was only my parents and my younger brother Loren and myself. The older siblings were already working at jobs outside the home as they were either in high school or graduated already.

This motel was in a big city in Ohio. It was right along the highway. But it had indoor plumbing. We could hear the traffic all night long. I remember my parents talking about the traffic for years afterwards.

The next day we visited some other cousins along the way in Pennsylvania. I met Aunt Lena, who was blind. I had never met or talked to a blind person before. I remember her feeling my face. What a strange sensation.

Her daughter, my cousin, sold AVON. I had no idea what AVON was, but she seemed like a nice lady. And then she gave me this pink jar. It was a cream sachet. She opened it and gently put some cream on my wrist. It smelled sweet. It was called Cotillion. It was my first perfume. My mother got some also.

My two sisters were not along on this trip so they were left out. That was the only time I met my Aunt Lena and my cousin Charlotte. She was my grandmother's sister and her daughter. I never knew my dad's mother or father. They both died many years before I was born.

After we visited these cousins we drove near Lake Erie and I saw grape vineyards for the first time. There was row after row after row. I had on my new spring program dress. The fabric was called Cracked Dice. It was bumpy. It had colored squares all over the white background. It was sleeveless. It was a wonderful summer dress and I loved getting my picture taken in it.

We stopped on the side of the road. We would take a picture of the vineyards. I ran down a row.

Snap. There I am standing in the grape orchard.

We climbed back into the car. Now we were on the way to my cousins in Niagara Falls. We were almost there.

There were cousins my age, second cousins or first cousins once removed. My dad was the second youngest son from a family of thirteen. The cousin whom we were visiting was the oldest daughter of the oldest sister. So the cousin and my dad who was her uncle were about the same age.

She also had a boy about my age. They also had a baby. We all had somebody to play with. This was much better than at the Minnesota farm. They seemed richer than we were. There were lots of toys.

Then we all piled into two cars and drove to Niagara Falls. It was only about a half-hour from their house. Wow! What a lot of water. It was fun running around with my cousin. I could buy a souvenir. It was hard to decide what to buy. I choose a wooden jewelry case that said Niagara Falls on it. In later years, I would see dozens of them in many tourist spots with the city name stamped on it. But for a ten-year-old child it was really special.

And then we saw the clock. It was fantastic. Everything except the hands was made out of flowers. That was a good spot to take a picture of the two young girl cousins. Snap, my dad took our picture. We promised to be friends forever.

In sad truth that visit was the only time I saw Joanne. I've seen her parents several times on visits back to Niagara Falls, but Joanne has moved away.

The other vacation trip I remember taking with my parents was when I was in high school. My dad liked to tour companies that made products. In grade school he arranged a trip for the students to tour a big bakery and also the canning factory where he had worked in the summer. Kellogg's and Post Cereals were both in Battle Creek, Michigan.

To make the trip even more special we drove over to Manitowoc where you could have your car put on ferry. The ride across Lake Michigan took over five hours. But that would still be faster than going down the western side of Lake Michigan, around Chicago and up into southern Michigan. And my dad knew that going on the ferry would be an adventure.

We could walk all over the ferry while we did the crossing. It moved very slowly. It was a cloudy day. But what fun it was to see all the different people on the ferry and walk around the upper and lower deck.

That evening we stayed in a motel near Battle Creek. The next day we got to see how corn flakes were made. At the end of the tour we were given samples of the different cereals the company made.

After the tour, we got in the car and a big thunderstorm came up. It rained so hard that my dad could not see in front of him. Many cars pulled on the side of the road. My dad stopped too. I don't know if I was more scared stopping in the car thinking that a tree could fall down on us, or driving and hoping that my dad could see okay to drive.

We were going on to Upper Michigan to visit his brother and his family and his sister and her husband. It seemed like a long drive. I wanted to read my book. I was told to watch the scenery. I said,

"It's just trees and more trees."

My parents weren't very happy with me, but let me continue my reading.

We needed to cross the Straits of Mackinaw. That was fun. It was a very big bridge. It was the biggest bridge that I had ever crossed. It was big enough for the big ships to go through from Lake Michigan to Lake Huron.

From there we drove up to Sault Ste. Marie, Canada. My dad wanted my brother and me to see the locks there. They were very important locks for commerce. It was also the Canadian and United States border.

I was more interested in reading my books than in looking at locks and trees.

It was late before we got to my uncle and aunt's house. They seemed liked nice people, but their children were all grown-up already. I didn't have any playmates. My dad and his brother visited and my mother had a chance to visit with her sister-in-law, but my brother and I had to entertain ourselves.

Maybe I was getting too old for vacations. Or maybe I was just getting too old to go on vacations with my parents. As it turned out, that was the last vacation I took with both of my parents. Soon I'd be off to college.

GRANDMA'S POTATO SALAD

10 – 12 medium size new potatoes
1 teaspoon salt
¼ teaspoon pepper
1 large yellow or other type of onion
8 slices bacon
½ cup mayonnaise
2 – 3 Tablespoons white vinegar

Boil potatoes leaving their skins on.
Boil until soft, but not mushy.
Cool.
Remove skins and slice potatoes.
Add salt and pepper to taste.
Peel and chop up onion.
Add onion.
Cut bacon in small pieces and fry until crisp.
Drain excess grease.
Leave a small amount for extra flavoring.
Add to potatoes.

Mix mayonnaise and vinegar and pour over potatoes.
Stir gently.
Chill.

Serves 10–12.

Nice late summer or autumn treat.

COUSINS

I had lots of cousins. I never knew them all. My dad had five sisters: Dora, Lydia, Hannah, Marie his twin, and Esther. Esther died from tuberculosis at age of eighteen. He always said she was the prettiest. My dad also had four brothers, three older than him: Ted or Theofeld, named after my grandfather, John and Andrew. The youngest in the family was Marcus.

Two additional children in the family died before the age of one. I know one was a girl named Tabea as it's recorded in the German family Bible. What a pretty name. All of the children that reached adulthood got married. Marcus was the only sibling that didn't have any children.

Between the siblings there were 52 grandchildren! My Aunt Marie married a minister and my Uncle Ted became a minister. Uncle John and Uncle Marcus became teachers in the Lutheran church. The siblings were scattered all over the United States.

The other sisters, Aunt Lydia and Aunt Hannah married farmers and lived in Wisconsin all their lives, while the other sister, Aunt Dora was in nearby Michigan. In later years the cousins lived in over half of the fifty states. There were doctors, lawyers, teachers and I'm sure many just ordinary folks.

I'm not sure how many second cousins are about, but my father alone had fourteen grandchildren. Lydia had over twenty grandchildren. So the Bible axiom of be fruitful and multiply was certainly taken to heart.

Even though I didn't live in the same farming community as my cousins I got to visit them fairly often. Fortunately most lived in the Midwest and several sets of cousins lived near my dad's childhood home. He loved to go down the old farm roads and tell us what it was like when he was a boy.

Unfortunately, my dad's dad died before he turned seven. His father was a Lutheran minister who had come over from the old country, the way Germany was always referred to by my relatives.

Mary Muehl, my grandmother grew up in Northeast, Pennsylvania. She was born in the United States. As a young woman, Mary, my grandmother, had traveled to South Dakota to keep house for her brother. While there she attended the Lutheran church where Theodore was the new young minister. They were married in Canastota, South Dakota in 1892.

My grandfather Theofield preached two services each Sunday, one German and the other English. My grandfather's death was from the flu caught from a cold. He went out after a Sunday service to visit a sick parishioner. He already had a cold and the Wisconsin spring was still cold and damp. He came home and took to bed. Within a week he died.

My grandmother was left with nine children to raise. The oldest daughter Dora was just turning twenty and the youngest Marcus was a babe in arms, not yet one.

As was the practice in most Lutheran parishes, the church provided the house for the minister's family. So it was that my grandparents, Theodore and Mary lived in a house owned by the church, commonly called the parsonage. Upon my grandfather's death, my grandmother, Mary was asked to leave the parsonage a few weeks after the funeral with her nine children. The youngest child was Marcus. He was still a toddler.

I don't ever remember my dad talking about these years. I know the oldest girls were sent out to find whatever jobs they could to bring in some money. Mayville, the nearby town where they moved, had several mills and canning factories. Perhaps they worked there. My grandmother took in laundry and sewing.

All five sons went on to college, although Andrew left college to help support his brother Ted get through the seminary. My dad at age 13 left Mayville for Milwaukee to attend the Lutheran high school as his preparation to become a Lutheran school teacher. John and Marcus also became teachers.

It was around this time that his sister closest to him in age, Esther, became ill and died shortly before her 20th birthday. I knew he was very fond of her. The older sisters were more like a mother to my dad. There was much sibling rivalry between my dad and his twin sister Marie. He always considered her smarter. In later years she would marry a minister and have eight children, all of whom became either doctors, ministers or lawyers.

I think his favorite brother was Marcus. They were nearest in age and lived together when they were both single young men. Marcus too loved to travel. In the 1930's he took off for California much to my dad's dismay. I've heard since, my dad felt he needed to stay in Wisconsin to look after his mother.

Why he didn't leave for California after his mother died, I don't know. My dad saw very little of Marcus and John after they moved to California. I remember several visits of John with his family to Wisconsin and my parents took a trip to California in the 1960's. Marcus and his wife never had any children. I met him and his wife Esther on a visit to California around 1961. His wife was extremely overweight, and died at a relatively young age. Marcus didn't stay in teaching, but worked in an airplane factory. He stayed in church work through his music, as he was an accomplished organist.

The brothers and sisters started a family round robin letter sometime after their Mother died. I know my dad looked forward to its arrival and many pictures and ideas were shared in this way.

My grandmother lived with my father until her death in 1933. She only knew of Lyle, my older brother's birth. I often wished as a child I had two sets of grandparents as many of my friends did.

Fortunately I got to know my mother's father, Grandfather Charles. Grandfather Charles was lots of fun and I loved him dearly. I could sit on his lap and snuggle up. His wife, my Grandmother, Louisa died when I was five. He liked to rub his whiskers on my face to make me giggle. He always sent his grandchildren two dollars for their birthday and often gave me a silver dollar when we saw him. I still have a few of them.

Grandfather Charles was not only a farmer, but also a carpenter. He built an early stone house and then a wonderful three-story frame house, barn and other farm buildings. He also built a beautiful teacher's desk for my dad out of oak, which my brother is now using and is more beautiful than ever. He also served on several township posts, could shoe horses and rode quite well.

It was Grandfather or his son, Uncle Clarence who taught my father how to ride a horse. Uncle Clarence and my dad became friends when my dad started tutoring one of his students at her home. This young student, Renata was a cousin to Clarence. On one of my dad's tutoring visits Clarence was there also. He invited my dad over to his folks farmhouse out in the country. Before long, Clarence's sister, Mildred and my dad, Martin were dating.

And so, by tutoring at the home of Renata my dad Martin met Mildred. The circle was joined. It would still be 14 years before I was in the picture, but the negative was made. Renata, the daughter of my grandfather's sister, and I still stay in touch with each other.

BANANA TEA LOAF

1 3/4 cups sifted flour
2 teaspoons baking powder
1/2 teaspoon baking soda
1 teaspoon salt
1/3 cup shortening
2/3 cup sugar
2 eggs
1 cup mashed bananas (2 - 3 ripe bananas)

Preheat oven 350 degrees.
Sift dry ingredients.
Cream bananas, sugar, eggs and shortening till very fluffy.
Blend all together well, but gently.
Turn into heavily buttered, floured loaf pan.
Bake 350 degrees for ONE hour.
Test with toothpick.
Continue baking anywhere from ten to twenty minutes longer until browning on edges.
Depends on the adjustment of the oven.
Chopped raisins, nuts or dates may be added.

Great way to use up ripe bananas.

BALL GAMES

My world was small growing up in rural Wisconsin. I dreamed of a wider world. I saw the outside world when my brother Lyle bought a television set. My sisters listened to the radio. I read a lot of books both from our school library and the public library in the town where my parents did their biweekly grocery shopping.

When I was about ten years old the Boston Braves moved to Milwaukee. Everyone in the neighborhood was excited about Milwaukee getting its own major league ball team. No longer would fans from Wisconsin have to root for the neighboring Chicago Cubs or Detroit Tigers. We would have a team of our own. It was wonderful to have our own team right in Milwaukee.

We lived one hundred miles from Milwaukee. My family didn't go to Milwaukee very often except for a special occasion.

My father had gone to high school in Milwaukee so he was acquainted with the major streets and roads. With the national highway 41 only about twenty miles from our house, we could be at the ballpark in a little over two hours. Most of the ball games were played in the day time, especially on the weekend, so we could pack a picnic lunch and head off for the park.

There was only one problem. My dad was the church organist, so Sunday was out and Saturday, well, he had to get ready for Sunday.

What could I do? I loved baseball. I loved the Braves. I knew all the players, listened to all the ball games on WTMJ day after day. I knew the batting average of all the players and who was leading in Runs Batted In (RBI's). When my brother-in-law asked me who was the Brave's top home run hitter, or who was their leading pitcher, I knew the answer. Hank Aaron and Eddie Matthews batted in the number three and number four slot for a number of seasons. I though Eddie Matthews was the greatest. He was good looking too. And for the pitchers they had Warren Spahn, Lew Burdette and Bob Buhl, a mighty trio. But, most of all I wanted to go to a ball game in person and not just listen to the games on the radio.

My brother had driven down to Chicago to see the Cubs play a few times, but I was just a little sister and too little for him to drag along to a ball game. By the time I was old enough to go along, he was married, raising a family and didn't have as much time for ball games.

And then, in reading our local newspaper, I saw an ad that said a special bus was going down to Milwaukee for some of the weekend games. The ad said that with one ticket, it would take care of transportation, lunch, a ticket to the ball game and the trip back home right after the game was over. This was all for $5.25. Well, I wanted to find somebody to go with me. Of course I'd consider going by myself and I did a few times. Usually though, I found a friend willing to give up a day for the Braves.

Wow! I was so happy.

My dad took me to the hotel in town where the bus was to pick up the fans at 10 AM. It must have been a summer weekday, for I would not have been allowed to miss church even for the Braves.

Even the ride on the bus was exciting. It was fun watching the world whiz by looking out the big bus window. The barns, the cows, the fields and pasture all passed by the window. There was not much industry to view down highway 41 from Appleton to Milwaukee, just cows and barns, cornfields and pasture. Black and white Guernsey cows mainly dotted the landscape. A few Holsteins and some Swiss dairy cows could be seen. They all gave white milk. The farmers loved to tease young girls, especially a teacher's kid. The farmers always tried to convince me that brown cows gave chocolate milk.

As the bus neared Milwaukee the highway got busier and there were more houses and fewer farms. Soon the bus filled with cheering fans would be there. The bus was filled with a mixture of people, young and old, all set to have a good time as they cheered for the Braves.

We entered the stadium together as we'd all be sitting in the same area. I splurged and bought a scorecard for fifty cents. I knew how to keep score. My brother had taught me how. The letter K was used for a strike, a K 3 for a swing strike, versus a KO for a called strike. I wrote down the visiting team's line-up. It was now time for the national anthem. Everyone in the stadium stood up. Everyone was to join in singing, "Oh say can you see…" This was glorious. This was a dream come true.

I don't remember if the Braves won or lost. I could look it up on my scorecard. I saved them all. What I remember is the excitement, the fans rooting and cheering, standing up, sitting down and the singing "Take me out to the ball games," during the 7th inning stretch. I loved all the colorful souvenirs and being part of the roaring crowd.

I was able to make several trips to see the Braves in the next few years.

On one trip I bought a red team pennant to hang on my bedroom wall. I couldn't believe that I had been in the same ballpark as Eddie Mathews, Hank Aaron and Warren Spahn. I thought I was dreaming.

One of the Milwaukee television stations carried a show called, "Ask the Braves." They invited questions from viewers. If your question was read on the air, you received a two dollar gift certificate for dry cleaning.

When the Braves were out-of-town the player's wives were on the panel. This was even better than the players. I could get a picture in my mind what they were like out-of-uniform.

I remember the night I was hoping my question would be asked. It was a Sunday night. There was a special program that included supper at church that I had to attend. I hadn't dared tell my family I wrote and sent in a question. I felt they would all laugh at me. My family couldn't understand why a girl was so crazy about baseball. I don't know either. I just liked it. The TV show started at 9 PM. If I left as soon as the supper and church program was over, and did not wait for the rest of my family, maybe I could see it. I ran home to watch the show.

Channel 6 didn't come in very good. We had an antenna with a router, but it couldn't get the weak signals. It was a cloudy, snowy picture. But, I could hear it. And sure enough my question was asked to Mrs. Eddie Mathews. I couldn't believe it. It was almost as good as meeting her in person. I was ecstatic. I think my family came home shortly after that and I told them. Their reaction was a typical, "Oh, Louise."

I was so happy. Now I'd write and join the Eddie Mathews fan club.

As time grew on, baseball became another one of my childhood memories. Maybe as time wore on, I just didn't have the time for it. I still enjoy going to a ballgame now and then. I feel bad that the Braves left Milwaukee. I never have felt a loyalty to the Brewers. Since I went to college in Chicago I became a Cubs fan. And it finally happened. I was able to see the Cubs win the National League pennant.

POTATO PANCAKES

6 medium potatoes
1 teaspoon salt
2 eggs
2 Tablespoons cream
2 Tablespoons flour

Grate potatoes.

Add the other ingredients, and fry over medium heat or in electric fry pan, 325 degrees.

It takes at least 5 minutes for each side.

After a few are fried, put on a pie plate or other Pyrex dish and place them in the oven on low heat to keep warm while frying the remaining pancakes.

Serve with applesauce and soup if desired.

Grandma's favorite.

WALL COLLAGE

Debbie Reynolds, Pat Boone, Grace Kelly and Rock Hudson were all my heroes and heroines. I never got to see many movies and yet the movie stars of the motion pictures were my lifeline to a fantasy world. I dreamed of the wonderful life I knew that they must lead. Fancy clothes, cars, dates galore, dancing under the stars. I figured they didn't fight, worry about money, or need to do the dishes, clean their room or other mundane chores an adolescent has to do.

I bought a subscription to "Photoplay" magazine. Wow! I looked for it to arrive in the mail each month. I would pore over it cover to cover. Several pictures were usually in color. After careful consideration I'd decide who to add to my wall collage.

My bedroom wall was covered with pictures of the latest movie stars. Sometimes I cut out the headlines that went with a photograph or made up my own. I carefully cut out the pictures or headlines that I wanted and using rubber cement stuck them up on my bedroom wall. My wall was painted light beige so with the colored pictures it made the room come alive. I sometimes used colored construction paper that my dad bought for school art projects to border the different photographs.

I also had some glossy black and white prints of some of the Milwaukee Braves baseball players. These I received when I ordered the annual report on the ball team from their public relations department.

Some months if I saved enough money I bought "Motion Picture" magazine at the five and dime store in Appleton. I never thought their pictures were of the same quality as "Photoplay," but I did love to read about their stories about movie stars marriages and the lives they led.

And then along came Elvis. Oh wow. I thought he was so wonderful. He spoke straight to me I thought. Because of him I sent in my first letter to our city newspaper.

It was about this time that Elvis Presley was making a name for himself. He became another hero to me much like Eddie Mathews. I read about him in the movie magazine, Photoplay, and looked for stories of him in my dad's newspaper. I especially remember seeing him on the Ed Sullivan show. I thought his music was grand.

WAPL, a radio station that played the popular tunes of the day had an announcer by the name of Bob Bandy. Now Bob was all right. He told a few jokes and thought he was funny. Every day about 12:20 he would play an Elvis song. I knew this, because I would have to come home from school to eat lunch. I would stay home until after the Elvis song was played.

Well, Bob Bandy didn't think much of Elvis. He played his records, but always had a nasty comment with it. He also thought he was a fad, and that his style of music wouldn't last long. There was a newspaper columnist who noted his comments. And this particular newspaper columnist agreed with

Bandy and generally thought the world was coming to an end with all this awful rock and roll music.

I had noticed that sometimes this columnist had letters in from local people commenting on his column. Well I thought, I'd write him a letter and tell him exactly what I thought of him and Bob Bandy. I thought they both were wrong. I told him that while I liked other music and I mentioned church music including Beethoven and Bach, I thought Elvis was good too. And that the way I saw it, I said I felt Elvis' music would probably last just as long as Beethoven's would! In my letter I mentioned that I thought Elvis was a lot better than either of them and that he'd be famous long after either of them were gone.

Much to my surprise my letter was printed, with a comment about how Elvis made strange bedfellows. I asked the newspaper not to put in my name. My family would be too embarrassed. I didn't tell my parents that I had written a letter.

But, to my surprise, my sister-in-law saw it in the paper. She brought a clipping of it over a few nights later, and said, "Is this your letter, Louise?" My face turned red. I was so embarrassed. I wanted to defend Elvis, but I didn't want to have to let my family see how strongly I felt about it.

Marlene figured it had to be me. She knew I adored Elvis and would defend him to the ends of the earth.

Once more, it was "Oh, Louise."

My parents never knew I did this, as I made her and my brother Lyle promise me that they wouldn't tell.

As I didn't have a record player in those years, I never bought an Elvis record until many years later. My dad had a 78 player and had some Mills Brothers records, along with Beethoven and some Fred Waring whom he liked.

I did buy sheet music though. My mother being a music teacher often had to stop at the music store in Appleton. The store would have a whole rack of different sheet music by the top artists. I saved up my money and bought one almost every time we went to town. This was about once a month. Each piece of sheet music costs forty cents.

I was so excited to get home and try out the new music. Sometimes the rhythm gave me a hard time, but I didn't care. I could pretend that I was playing it as good as it sounded on the radio.

My parents were happy that I was playing piano, even if it wasn't classical or church music.

And I still enjoy listening to Elvis music.

CUCUMBER SALAD

Peel 3 - 4 large cucumbers.
Slice thinly.
Place in medium size bowl.
Sprinkle 1 – 2 teaspoons salt on top.
Cover with glass plate that fits against cucumbers.
Let sit 2 – 3 hours.
Drain off excess liquid.
Add 1 – 2 Tablespoons white vinegar
Add 2 – 3 Tablespoons sugar
Mix well.
Chill.

Nice side summer salad.

WEDDINGS

Being the fourth out of five children did have its advantages. When I was younger I know I didn't see it that way, but looking back in time I know that it's true.

For one thing, I grew tired of hearing that I would be able to do something when I got older. It always seemed to me that they had the advantage. My sisters were allowed to stay up later for one thing. I always felt I was missing out on something when I got sent to bed early.

They also got to go places that I couldn't go, like drive-in movies. I was told I was too little. "Why not let me just sleep in the car," I would ask. And then my sister got a job down in Chicago for the summer taking care of children. Now wouldn't that be fun. She also got to use the family car. My dad didn't even allow me to use our car most of the time.

And then before I knew it my oldest sister was getting married. That seemed so grown-up. She was getting married and here I was only ten years old. I knew the guy she was marrying. He just lived up on the next farm. I played with his younger sister all the time. We would play "Weddings" all the time.

They lived in a big farm house. Her mother had a bunch of old lacy curtains. She let Shirley and me play with them. We pretended that we were all grown up and getting married. We made up names of men that we would marry. Sometimes we pretended we were getting married to movie stars, or sometimes baseball players.

In the upstairs at the farmhouse was a long hallway. That would be our church aisle. We would hum, "Here comes the bride." We would have the lacy curtains wrapped around us. Sometime we had a double wedding, and sometimes we took turns and one of us would be the maid of honor.

In the summer we would play in back of our house out by the garage. We really didn't want anyone to see us. It was all pretend, but grown-ups sure like to tease younger people, so it was better to do the pretending in an out-of-the-way spot.

After we got married we always had babies. We both used our dolls. We dressed them up, baptized them and took them for buggy rides. Grown ups seemed to expect young girls to play with doll babies, but they didn't seem to think of us as getting married. Yet we knew that you had to be married to have children.

Then one day my sister and her brother were getting married for real. We were both so excited. We knew there were a lot of plans to be made. Her brother had to go in the army. There was not enough time to plan the wedding before he had to leave for the army. The wedding would have to wait awhile.

My sister was now working in the neighboring big city as a secretary. She was able to get a ride in to work with the neighbor man who also worked in the city for the insurance company. He was just a young man with two young children. It was fun to play at their house. As I got older I also got to baby-sit there.

Shirley and I were both so excited. We weren't old enough to be regular bridesmaids and we were too old to be flower girls, so my sister decided that we could stand up together and be junior bridesmaids.

My next older sister LeAnne would be the matron of honor. She would stand up with Shirley's only brother, Gordon. Otto's two sisters, Vera and Ardella would be bridesmaids. My older brother Lyle would be a groomsman and Otto's brother-in-laws, Frank and Art, would be ushers. Our younger brother Loren would get a new suit, but he didn't get to be in the wedding party.

As Otto had to leave for the army they couldn't get a date set right away. They figured it would be in the winter. We could start shopping for our dresses. We went to Appleton and tried on dresses. I had never had a formal dress before. Deep winter colors were picked. Shirley and I would wear dark green dresses. They would be long and trimmed with velvet. My sister would have a dark red velvet dress. The neckline was scooped and a tight cummerbund at the waist with a long flowing satin skirt covered with matching netting. The other two bridesmaids had pretty sky blue fabric for their dresses. As the dresses were long and covered our shoes, we would all buy new shoes, but the shoes wouldn't be dyed to match. We could all just buy new black patent Sunday dress shoes. In our hair a small net-like hat was made to match our dress color.

My sister went shopping for her wedding dress with my mother. My mother had saved her piano money to help pay for all these expenses. The wedding dinner would be down in the church basement. The women from the church would help serve. My mother and sister planned the food. There would also be a reception at Otto's parents farmhouse. It was a big house. It was near the church, so people wouldn't need to drive far.

Otto found out later that fall that he could get a weekend leave probably in December. By then the weather could get quite cold in Wisconsin. But they didn't want to wait until springtime, so they thought they would take a chance and hope for a warm December.

It turned out to be the weekend before Christmas. It was a busy time. My dad was busy in school preparing for the church Christmas program. My mother always sewed the three of us girls new Christmas dresses. My mother also always had piano lessons and was busy making her waxed roses.

My sisters did a lot of the work. They cleaned the house thoroughly as relatives would be stopping in before or after the wedding. The Christmas tree was put up. A special wedding cake was ordered and special flowers for walking down the aisle and to decorate the church.

My sister had to pick up the flowers the morning of the wedding. The weather had turned bitter cold. She couldn't get a parking spot real close to the florist, and as she carried them back to the car some of the blossoms froze.

Wearing my long dress to church was very special. We had to make several trips in the family car. My coat wouldn't fit because of all the crinolines under the nettings. It covered my shoulders, but oh it was cold.

It was so exciting. The church was filled with family, friends and many relatives from far and near. The neighbor lady sang. She had a lovely voice. My sister asked a friend to be her organist so that my dad could walk her down the aisle. It was all very exciting to me a ten-year-old younger sister.

After the church service, we had our pictures taken in front of the altar. Then we went downstairs to have dinner. My grandfather was there too.

After everyone had eaten they were invited to go the groom's house where they would open all the presents. They had a bar set up down the basement. Shirley and I were not allowed to have any beer, but we really didn't care. We were treated special because we were the junior bridesmaids.

It was a very special day.

My sister still had to live at home for a few months until her husband finished all his special training. They wrote letters back and forth every day. Then he got transferred again, and was finally allowed to live off base and bring his wife. He found an apartment for them about ten miles from the base.

My sister was going to have to move away. Even though it was only for a short time it would seem much longer. We had all always lived together. Now we would be one less.

Telephone calls were much more expensive in those days. To keep in touch everyone wrote letters. My sister wrote to my mother and dad every day. I usually wrote her once a week. It was fun getting letters. I always had to write to my grandfather too. Sometimes it was hard to think of any special news to write to her about.

Then in one letter my sister wrote my mother that she was expecting a baby. This was exciting news. The baby was due the following winter, around Christmas time. They would still be living far away near the army base.

Lyle, my older brother was out working. He owned his own car, a Plymouth coupe. He suggested to my mother that we could go visit my sister and her husband. He could drive. He was twenty-two years old. He had to arrange to get off from work. My dad wasn't able to go as he always had the organ to play and school would be starting soon.

It was decided that my mother, sister and two brothers would go. We would leave early in the morning and drive until we got there. It was over seven hundred miles. He drove and drove. My brother loved to drive his new car. It was a small car for the five of us.

When we got to North Carolina it was nighttime. It was so good to see my sister and her husband. We made up beds on the floor. My mother slept on their sofa.

We did some sightseeing in the area. We saw where the autumn before Hurricane Hazel had come through and torn out homes and trees along the ocean. We have a picture of us children standing by some of the big roots of the trees that were blown out of the ground.

Soon it was time for us to drive back. Otto was able to get a couple of extra days of leave and we made plans to visit Washington D.C. together. Both he and Lyle would drive their cars.

We followed each other in the cars and switched passengers around. We would spend one night in a motel in Washington D.C. This would be the first visit for all of us.

We did not expect so much traffic. As we got closer to the city traffic got very heavy. All of a sudden we lost sight of each other. What were we to do? We hadn't decided on a meeting spot and we didn't know the city.

We just kept driving towards the city and towards the special monuments. Then all of a sudden, my brother hollered, "There they are." Otto had pulled aside off the road by a motel hoping he would see us pass. We met up again. We shook our heads in amazement. How easy it was to lose each other in a big city. After this we were more careful and made special arrangements if we got lost in traffic.

We parked the cars near the Washington Monument. It was so big and tall. We stood and gazed at it. Could we walk up it? My mother thought my sister shouldn't do it because she was pregnant, so she waited down below with her and my younger brother Loren. The rest of us raced on ahead.

It had over a thousand steps to the top where you could gaze and look out over the entire city. What a wonderful view I saw while looking down below. The cars looked so small. The people looked so small. I could see all the beautiful monuments and memorials, and also the Capitol. It was spectacular.

After climbing the monument we drove to the Lincoln Memorial. That was breathtaking. Lincoln looked so big sitting there in his chair. I had my camera with me. We took lots of pictures. I ran out of film and was able to buy some from a stand set-up nearby. I couldn't believe how pretty the city looked.

It was time to find a motel for the night. We would have to rent two rooms. This was a very special trip. We had to eat dinner out. Then it was time for bed.

The next morning it was decided that we would go in one of those taxis that hired themselves out for a tour of the city. We wanted to find one that would let us all ride together. Loren and I sat on laps.

We toured for five hours. We went to the mint and watched where they made the money for the United States. We went on a tour of the capitol building and visited some of the Smithsonian buildings. We saw the old flag which inspired Francis Scott Key to write the Star Spangled Banner. We had hoped to go into the White House but the line was too long. So we just walked by it. We also went in the FBI building and heard all about how their agents catch the criminals.

It was an exciting day.

Then it was time to say goodbye to my sister and her husband. We weren't sure when we would see them again, but probably not before she had the baby.

They had to drive back to North Carolina and Otto would finish his army tour of duty. We had to drive back to Wisconsin. Lyle thought we could do it in one long drive. My mother thought we should maybe stop one night.

We drove and drove. We fell asleep. My brother kept driving. I woke up when we reached the city lights of Chicago. Would we stop in Chicago and stay in a motel? No, my brother thought we were so close to home he might as well keep driving. It was another two-hundred miles. Lyle was the only one who had a driver's license. He would have to do all the driving. He didn't mind. He loved to drive.

I stayed awake for a while and talked to him, but as soon as the city lights faded away I got too sleepy and fell back asleep. I don't remember what time it was when we got home, but I know it was about midnight when we were in Chicago.

It was a long, long day but what a wonderful trip. It was so good seeing LaVerne. It seemed all different seeing my sister in her own house with her husband Otto. She seemed so grown up.

Now it was just my sister LeAnne and I sharing the bedroom. It did give us more space. But we sure missed LaVerne.

In just two years more changes would be coming to our family.

And before that, we got news on New Years Day that my sister had a baby boy. They named him Michael. I was an aunt. My mother and dad were grandparents. Were they really that old?

My grandfather was a great-grandfather. That made him really old. LaVerne and Otto came back to Wisconsin the following May. It was then that we saw their baby son Michael for the first time. He was so cute. It was so good to have them nearby again.

I was able to visit them often and help my sister take care of the baby. It was fun being a little sister now, because I was grown up enough to be a babysitter, not just a baby sister.

It wasn't long though that more changes were coming to our family. My oldest brother Lyle was out working in a big paper mill in the city. He was learning how to run the big printing presses. When he had some time off he would go out with his buddies. Because he had had rheumatic fever when he was eighteen he was ineligible to join the U.S. Army. He was quite disappointed. Many of his friends were going off into the Army.

Then one spring day he told my mother he'd like to bring a girl over for Sunday dinner. This was a big surprise. He hadn't told us he was dating anyone. We thought he was always just out with the guys.

It was Easter Sunday. LaVerne and Otto were still down in North Carolina. My mother prepared her special Sunday dinner. She fixed a roast chicken and stuffed it with seasoned bread crumbs. She had mashed potatoes and gravy and fresh corn. The corn was from our garden the summer before and had been frozen in our big deep chest freezer. My mother also made a special chocolate cake and served it with ice cream.

Lyle's girl friend was named Marlene. She had pretty short blond hair. She had a lovely smile and a quiet laugh. I could see why Lyle liked her. She was so nice.

Soon Marlene was visiting our house more often. Lyle brought her to the church picnic. And before long they were talking about getting married.

My parents, my brother and I were invited over to meet Marlene's family. She lived in the nearby town of Oshkosh. She had graduated from high school and worked as a secretary. She had three older sisters and one older brother.

Lyle and Marlene decided to get married in the summer. My sister LaVerne and her husband Otto, with the new baby would be back in Wisconsin by then. As Marlene had older sisters, and I was just twelve, I was not going to be in the wedding party. My mother sewed me a new yellow dress. It was a sheer nylon fabric that she lined with taffeta. I had a new pair of white shoes. Marlene's friends had a wedding shower for her and I was invited to that. I felt very grown up.

Several weeks before the wedding my grandfather Charles became sick. He was taken to the hospital. My mother went to see him. In only a few days he died. I felt sad. It was always fun to have him visit. He liked to tease me.

We went to the funeral. He was living with my Uncle Clarence and his family. I knew people died when they got old, but I wish my grandfather had not gotten sick. He was my friend and I liked talking to him. Even though everyone was sad, the wedding plans had all been made and it was decided that my grandfather would not want Lyle to postpone his wedding.

Wisconsin sometimes gets very hot in July and August. The farmers are happy about it because it made the corn grow, especially if there was enough moisture in the air. It did not feel very good to me when I had to get all dressed up in my new dress. It was hot and sticky. I had just started wearing nylons and I decided it was too hot to wear them on such a sweltering summer day. Luckily my hair was cut short and I wore it straight. With the weather being so hot and humid my hair would go straight even if I had set it in curlers. It seemed everyone was talking about the hot weather.

After the church service and the dinner there was a dance. Lyle and Marlene danced with each other. My dad wasn't too happy about it, but as the bride's parents planned the wedding and Lyle and Marlene wanted a dance, my dad acquiesced. Dad didn't dance though. He spent his time visiting with relatives and friends. I don't remember my parents ever dancing together. I wonder if they ever did.

Lyle and Marlene drove to Niagara Falls for their honeymoon. After they came back they rented an apartment in Neenah where my brother worked at the paper presses. I looked forward when they came to visit. Sometimes they came in the evenings, and sometimes they came on Sundays and went to church with us.

Before long, Marlene told us that she was expecting a baby. I was going to be an aunt again. My sister was also expecting another baby. It was fun being a younger sister. I especially liked when I could visit their homes and stay over night. It made me feel grown up and I felt that I could talk to them and that they understood me better than my parents did. I knew I was lucky to have them around.

After the babies were born I was old enough to baby-sit. It was fun holding and babies and taking them for rides in their strollers. Most of my friends were not aunts yet, so I felt very fortunate.

And before long, my next older sister LeAnne was graduating from high school. She had been planning on going to college. But, then she started dating a neighbor boy who had already graduated from college. He was also a good friend of my brother's so we all knew him and his family very well. It was fun teasing them. It seemed strange to me that they would be dating. I just had seen him as a friend of my brother's who liked to play ball and hang around the house. He was quiet, but easy to talk to. Before long, my sister received a diamond engagement ring. Soon another wedding was being planned.

I was now thirteen years old. My sister said I could be a bridesmaid. Wow. I was so excited. This meant that I would stand up with a man. I couldn't believe it. I had not dated. I was not in high school yet. Even if my dad would have allowed me to I couldn't imagine who would go out with me. But, to stand up with a guy in a wedding was special. I felt so grown up.

They decided on a spring wedding. We went shopping for gowns. They would be full, but not down to the floor. We would have matching high heeled shoes. This was my very first pair of high heels. We also bought matching full-brimmed hats. I would be standing up with my sister's new brother-in-law Gerald. My sister LaVerne and brother Lyle were also standing up, but again my younger brother Loren was not the right age. He was about nine years old, too old to be a ring-bearer and too young to be groomsman. I was so excited about being in the wedding, I never asked him if he felt left-out.

My sister loved to have a sun tan. Wisconsin does not usually get an early spring. It was hard to get a sun tan by early May. But try we did. Any time that it was sunny the last two months before the wedding, we crawled out of our bedroom window and lay on the roof. It had a slight slant to it, but not too steep to fall off. Of course we could only do this on the weekends. My sister was now working as a secretary at the big local paper mill in town. Her husband-to-be, Willard, was a civil engineer and had a job with the Wisconsin state highway department.

It was a beautiful wedding day, not too hot and not too cold. They were married in the early evening. The reception was at a hall in the nearby town of New London where I went to high school. I could tell my dad was becoming mellow as he allowed my sister to have a dance. He did not dance, but stayed at the wedding to watch the bride and groom dance.

I was treated like a grown up. I got to go with the bridal party to the bar and had a mixed drink. I had a good time with all my friends and got to dance in my full bouffant dress. After a while I kicked off my heels and had an easier time swirling on the dance floor.

I helped carry the presents to the car. They were going to be opened after they came back from their honeymoon. They planned to drive all the way to Mexico. That was a long drive from Wisconsin. They were gone for three weeks.

I was excited because I was going to have the bedroom all to myself. I had always shared the bedroom with first my two sisters, LaVerne and LeAnne, then with LeAnne, and now I would have it all by myself. No one would be telling me to pick up my clothes, or not to snore, or go to sleep. I would have the bedroom all to myself.

It wasn't long before I realized that I missed LeAnne. I had no one to talk to in the evenings. I had no one to tell my ideas too. My brother Loren was there, but he was only nine. What did he know? My sisters told me stuff. They helped me learn about clothes and hair and guys and make-up. What did a kid brother know about those things?

My life was changing. My sisters still lived close by, but they were now busy with their husbands and new families. Growing up brought many changes, and at times I wished I could go back and be a little girl again.

ANISE SUGAR COOKIES

1/2 cup butter
1 egg
1 Tablespoon hot water
1 cup sugar
3/4 teaspoon baking soda
4 Tablespoons milk
2 1/2 cups flour
1/2 teaspoon anise oil or any flavoring

Mix butter, sugar, egg and water together.
Add soda to sour milk.
Add to mixture alternating with flour.
Make dough into a ball and place on a floured board.
Use additional flour if necessary.
Roll as thin as possible.
Using Christmas or other holiday cookie cutters. cut into shapes.
Bake 12 - 15 minutes at 350 or 375 degrees.
Sprinkle with colored sugar or ice with vanilla frosting tinted in color as desired.

Good anytime of year, but especially fun for Christmas.

THE BUS RIDE

Long before the idea of "busing" became a political ball game rural students were bussed to school.

For my grade school years I was fortunate. Even though we lived in a very rural area of Wisconsin our house was only about a tenth of a mile from school and I could easily make it to school on my bicycle in a few minutes. Even walking took less than ten minutes if I didn't dawdle along the way.

But high school was a different story.

Very few rural communities had the resources to provide a high school education for their own area students. Only by communities going together and connecting to a larger town could an adequate four year high school education be provided to its students.

Thus I went to New London for high school. This was a town of about 5,000 people located twelve miles away taking the direct car route. In a rural community there are many side roads and village roads. The school bus must pick up all the students from hither and yon. Over all New London had twenty buses collecting its students and the ride rather than taking about twenty minutes like in a car took over an hour.

The school bus would stop at a student's house, and then start again, go maybe one mile or a half mile and stop at the next house, wait often a minute or two, then start up again for the next pick-up. Down this road, up that hill, around that curve, mothers running out waving the bus on if a student was sick, or running out and asking the bus driver, "please wait, she's coming." The school district rule was that the bus driver needed to wait only three minutes at any one stop.

It was many the morning I tore out of the house, with socks in hand, or my slip in my lunch bag, or worst yet, no lunch at all. Never, no never, though, would I miss the bus and have the possibility of my dad driving me in. He just wouldn't consider it. He had his own school students arriving at his school. And my mother, well, my dad didn't want her to get a license. He didn't think it was necessary. He was the man of the house.

Eventually though he gave in, as after all, he let his two daughters drive and his eldest son. It was right before my mother's 50th birthday. So, when I got my license right after I turned sixteen, my mother got her driver's license also

Somehow I never managed to allow myself five extra minutes in the morning and so was always running out the door, a habit I guess I picked up from my sisters.

I had a real system though. When my music started playing on my radio alarm clock, I woke up, got dressed quickly and I was ready to go downstairs within ten minutes before the loud buzzer alarm went off. The alarm was my signal to be ready for my turn in the bathroom. There I washed my face, brushed my teeth, squeezed some cream on my face, added a little make-up, eye brow pencil and yanked the rollers out of my hair. Ouch, oh, why did I have to sleep on those miserable things? Oh, I know why I did it, I wanted to be beautiful! Then I quickly brushed my hair. Some days I wondered if being beautiful was worth all that fuss and bother.

Six minutes later I was gulping down a dish of cereal and bread was in the toaster. I gulped down a quick glass of milk and there was the bus. My mother handed me my lunch. I grab an unbuttered piece of toast, grabbed my books off the freezer and I was out the door. This was all in less than twenty minutes since my radio alarm went off.

Once on the bus, I usually found a seat by myself so I spread out my school assignments for a few minutes. If I had no schoolwork to finish I sat down by a friend. The first half hour or so most of us students were busy finishing up our homework.

I learned to write over the bumps and jostles and concentrate over the constant din of noise of the guys in the back of the bus who were always horsing around.

After awhile, talk began. First we talked about any new guys one of us girls might have a crush on. Then we'd discuss who was dating whom, or what was on television last night. Or perhaps, we'd talk about a meeting at school. Sometimes we quizzed each other on tests coming up, or discussed teachers. Rarely was politics a topic, only in my junior and senior year with the new boy in town.

He always wanted to discuss issues. He seemed so smart. I never knew quite what to say. I never had to think so much on my own. Stan, although sometimes a pest, was always nice to me and became a good friend. His parents were very strict Catholics, so even if we had thought of dating, we didn't dare. He did often bring me home from basketball games or school activities as his dad allowed him to take the family car, a privilege I seldom had. It was an Edsel.

I always took a full schedule of classes. I really liked history and English, as I loved to read and didn't mind writing assignments. Science was a bit harder as I never could quite understand all the formulas and pronounce the scientific terms.

Algebra and geometry were easy for me. Latin was interesting, but dull in my viewpoint. I also had physical education three times a week and I always found that fun, even though the clothing I had to wear for class made me look like a duck.

In high school I joined many activities. I wrote for the high school newspaper, joined the library club, intramural sports, forensics, FHA (Future Homemakers of America), and thespians.

Through these activities I was able to make many friends. One of my best friends was Sharrey. Her home became my second home. Her parents were warm and wonderful and always made me feel a part of the family. Her dad worked for a big bakery in Appleton, the nearby big city, and so on the nights that I slept over at Sharrey's house, we would be sure to have some fresh pastry for breakfast. What a special treat that seemed to me.

Sharrey also had a lot of sleepovers inviting five, six sometimes even ten other girls. What fun that was. This was usually on a Friday night after a basketball game. We'd go to the game together, some of us playing in the jazz band. Then there was a "sock hop" afterwards. Usually, the girls ended up dancing with each other and the boys would be standing on the sidelines watching us girls dance. But, we didn't care. Most of them were too short for us anyway.

After the dance a group of us girls walked over to Sharrey's house. It was about a fifteen minute walk. We'd all get ready for bed, taking turns in the bathroom, as there was only one bathroom. Some of us set our hair in rollers, depending on what was on the calendar for Saturday. Once we were all ready for bed, we got out the blankets and spread them all over the living room floor. And then we talked and giggled for a good part of the night.

It was in those all night discussions that we discussed religion. We came from a variety of backgrounds. All of my friends attended church. I had Methodist, Lutheran, Catholic or Reform religions among the friends in my group. We couldn't understand our parent's big hang up about only one church being right. We all believed in God.

We all knew the story of Jesus on the cross. At this time, none of us were acquainted with girls in the Jewish faith, although we knew that they believed in God. It seemed a shame that religion seemed to divide some people rather than bring them closer together.

Usually I had arranged for my parents to pick me up either at Sharrey's house, or somewhere in town on Saturday morning. They often had to come to New London to do the major grocery shopping, and my dad had to pick up school supplies. Sometimes my mother purchased some fabric to sew a new dress for one of us children.

My sister, who was in high school ahead of me, had joined the band and played the French horn. Because of her work schedule in the summer she never was able to take a trip with the band.

Well, I just figured I would join the band too and play an instrument. I really wanted a different one than what she played, but the band needed another French horn player, so French horn it was. Fortunately, the school would rent any student an instrument for four dollars a year. My parents couldn't afford to buy me one.

As I knew how to play the piano, I didn't have too much trouble learning how to play the horn. My main problem was learning how to do the off beat notes. The horn usually didn't get the melody, but had the background instrumentation. My horn came home with me every night and I would practice counting 1 and, 2 and, over and over again.

Most of the students in band had taken band in junior high. I had piano lessons so I knew how to read notes, but I had never played with another person except occasionally a duet on the piano, or when I accompanied our church choir on the organ. So in my first year, I played quietly so that my wrong notes wouldn't be heard.

Early in the fall it was announced that our band was chosen to represent Wisconsin at the Lion's Club Parade next summer in New York City. Wow! I couldn't believe it. I was going to get a chance to go to New York City. I was in heaven.

The band director announced that we not only would have to do a lot of practice marching, but also raise the money in order for all of us to participate. Many ideas were talked about what we could sell to help raise the money.

If each of us met our quota, it would end up costing us very little and all of us would get a chance to not only go to New York City, but Gettysburg and Washington D.C. There were about seventy students in the band and we were all determined to go.

I remember selling boxes and boxes of light bulbs. I also sold candy, fruit, cards, stationary and assorted other items. The most ingenious item that was sold were "chances" or tickets at a quarter a piece. The prize would be a transistor radio that was donated by a local shopkeeper. These were hot new items back in the late fifties. The trick was to guess when the Wolf River would have its first thaw. The person had to write down the date and time that they thought the ice would melt. Chances were a quarter a piece. It didn't seem very likely to me that anyone could guess with much chance of winning, but the person closest to the date that the ice went out would be the winner. There was a marker on the ice, and when that sunk you knew the ice was melting.

I sold a number of chances, and some people bought several and wrote down a different date and time on each one. I sold one chance to my brother-in-law. And, much to both his and my surprise, he was the winner. It was a good hardy transistor radio that he had for years, all for a quarter.

The trip ended up costing each student $36.00. This was for the bus trip to New York City, hotel and most meals. It also included two nights in Washington, D.C. and with that the opportunity for us students to play on the capital steps.

While I was enjoying the fund-raising, I was having trouble marching. I had never marched before. Getting the syncopation, plus playing the music really gave me a hard time. A good friend and fellow horn player Janet helped a lot, and I found myself counting more than playing.

We had special practices in the summer before our big trip. Then, one night after practice the band director came over and talked to me. This was a big parade and that the band would be judged by how well it did. He was still concerned about my marching in step. He wanted me to go on the trip as I had worked as hard as all the other students, but would I mind if I didn't march down 5th Avenue? I didn't know what to say. I had to swallow my pride. I was all excited about going to New York City. Would it matter that I didn't march? I really wanted to march. The band director said I could walk with the assistant band director, who also wouldn't be in uniform. I could wear my uniform for the other events as the band would also be playing at Madison Square Garden and on the capitol steps and in Gettysburg.

I was the new kid on the block, so it did seem to me that the other band students understood. My other concern was who would be my roommate at the hotel. They were reserving rooms for four. There were four good friends from junior high all going on the trip and they had already talked about rooming together. Once more, I was the new kid on the block. I ended up rooming with several juniors, kind of like the leftover partners. Most of our activities were as a group so it didn't really present a problem other than to my pride. I had really wanted to room with my classmates, but the rule was firm, only four to a room.

There would be two big chartered buses going to New York City. All the instruments and uniforms had to go with us. Most of the band students were on the same bus. It was loaded before dawn. We were on the road by 5:30 AM. We would be driving all of one day and one night. It was a fun exciting time.

Singing and playing word games was the main activity on the bus. We'd all pile out at the rest stops. I can still remember my first sight of New York City. It was awesome to see all the big tall buildings. It was even more spectacular than I had hoped. We got to take a boat trip around Manhattan and went to see Robert Preston in "The Music Man." We played at Madison Square Garden and got to see the Rockettes at Radio City Music Hall. I walked down Broadway. I planned to buy souvenirs for mom and dad. I thought it would be neat to buy my dad a new pair of swimming trunks. I went into a store to price them. I looked and looked. I had about three dollars in my wallet. A clerk came over to see if I needed some help. I told him about wanting to buy my dad a pair of swimming trunks, but I couldn't find any for three dollars. He said, "Let's see what we can do." He found a pair for five dollars.

"Sorry, I don't have any more money with me. Maybe I can borrow some from a friend." He said, "Not to worry." He would put in the rest of the money. I was so surprised. He said he wanted to do it, so that I would remember that there were indeed nice people in New York City. I've never forgotten.

The band made it to Washington D C. where we got to meet our local representative. We were presented with a flag to take back to New London and our band played on the Capitol steps. Our picture was taken and the story appeared in our local newspaper. After Washington, D.C. we stopped in Gettysburg for one day and went on a tour of the battlefield. Again we had our picture taken, which appeared in our local newspaper. After that, I think most of us slept all the way back to Wisconsin. It was a fun packed eight days and my best bus trip ever.

FRESH BROCCOLI SALAD

Broccoli 3-4 small heads
2/3 cup green olives, chopped
1 small onion, grated or chopped
4 hard boiled eggs, chopped
1 cup mayonnaise
1 Tablespoon lemon juice
½ teaspoon sugar
Salt and pepper to taste
Fresh mushrooms, sliced.

Cut broccoli, including stalks into cubes.
Add olives, onion and chopped eggs.
Combine mayonnaise, lemon juice, sugar, salt and pepper.
Toss with broccoli mixture.
Garnish with fresh mushrooms or add them to broccoli mixture.
Serves 6 – 8, depending on amount of broccoli.

Fun way to serve broccoli.

JFK'S VISIT

My entrance to politics came the day John Fitzgerald Kennedy visited my high school. I was a junior the year JFK ran in the Wisconsin primary election. My world history teacher was the president of the Young Democrats of Wisconsin. I thought the world of my history teacher. He was in fact, the first real Democrat I knew. My parents were both Republicans as were most of the Lutherans in our tightly knit German community.

But when John F. Kennedy came to our high school to talk I was mesmerized. He was so charming and so young. All the politicians I had ever seen were old men. Dwight Eisenhower was the President of the United States during most of my grade school years, and Ike as he was nicknamed by the press and his wife Mamie, appeared like very old grandparents to me.

Living out in the country, as did over half of the high school student population, we rode bright yellow school buses to and from school. Many of us were on the bus over two hours a day. To get the students home on time, the bus schedule was paramount. Students had to get home in time to help with evening chores, and the high school didn't want frantic mothers calling in with worry or dads upset that their sons weren't home in time to help with the evening chores. So before Senator Kennedy finished speaking, the announcement came across the speaker system that all the bus Children had to leave the assembly to catch their buses.

Well, I didn't care. I'd miss that bus. I wanted to hear more from this spellbinding person.

Well, then he announced that he didn't realize that he had run over in time so he said he would take just a few more questions and call it a day. The day was saved. Most everyone sat down again and a few more questions were asked. Then there was a mad rush for the doors and buses.

But wait, maybe I could get his autograph. Our school newspaper was handed out right before the assembly so it was in my hand. I rushed forward to be near him coming down the aisle.

He smiled at me. I melted. He shook my hand, asked me my name and wrote, "To Louise, J. F. Kennedy." Wow. I would cherish it forever.

Sad to say, the School Daze, the school newspaper, got put on a shelf in the closet with a stack of lots of other school papers. When my parents moved and I was already married all those papers got thrown out. I was heartsick. I was really upset with my mother. But she didn't know and of course she didn't know how much I really liked JFK.

I was too young to vote and everyone in my family who voted was for Nixon. My one sister really thought Nixon was handsome. I found that hard to believe.

Well, what's done is done. The memory still lingers and I did say "Hello" to him. I did shake his hand and he did smile at me.

The weekend of the assassination I was a sophomore in college. I was dumbstruck. He was my hero. People don't kill their heroes, their President. What was that all about? I was glued to the television all weekend. I bought every Chicago paper I could find. I bought the magazines. I couldn't read enough about how it all happened, his life, his wife and their children. That weekend started a new political awareness of the world I lived in. Heroes lived real lives. Camelot was only in the movies. Heroes are real people who have enemies. Heroes are not protected from death.

The following week was semester finals at college. I did poorly. I couldn't concentrate. How could life go on? But seeing Jackie and little Jon saluting the flag helped me realize that life went on. Their children lost their father, she lost her husband and all of us lost our President.

That weekend the turmoil of the sixties began. I realized my childhood and the fantasy world of my childhood was over.

GRANDMA'S GOULASH

Cut round steak, or other beef, into bite-size pieces
Season with salt and pepper.
Cut a medium onion over steak.
Melt vegetable shortening in fry pan.
Add meat and onion.
Sauté.
Peel 3 – 4 potatoes and cut into bite size pieces.
Pour 2 cups tomato juice over and add potatoes.
Add more juice as desired.

Family favorite.

LYLE

Maybe because he was the oldest of my siblings, or maybe because he was my only older brother, or maybe because he just let me be and didn't tease me like my two older sisters did, or scold me like my dad did, for whatever the reason I always felt that my older brother was special. I'd do anything to please him.

He was eleven years older than I was. When I was a child of four and five, having a brother fifteen and sixteen makes him seem much older. He was driving a car before I learned how to ride a bike. He was working on a neighbor's farm for the summer when I was learning how to read. He seemed to me to be so much older and wiser.

I already told the story of how Lyle helped me to learn how to ride my two-wheeler. It was so big, I was certain that I would never learn how to balance it. Lyle walked with me next to the big bike, helping me get the idea of balancing it. Before I knew it, by the end of the afternoon I could ride up and down our driveway.

Some years later after he was married already, Lyle took the time to help me learn how to drive the car. My dad was too impatient and expected me to just know what to do. I remember one afternoon, when I had gone to the neighboring town with my dad I talked him into letting me drive the car home. We had to be on a major highway for about two miles. I knew where the turnoff was to our country road. I had bicycled on it many times. As I was just getting near the turn, my dad reached over me and yanked on the emergency brakes. He thought I wouldn't stop in time. Fortunately, no cars were behind us and we didn't have an accident. But, my dad always thought he knew best.

Lyle, on the other hand, would let me drive along and then if I was to do something, he would say in a very quiet way, "Were you planning to go on County W?" In his own quiet way, he let you know what to do, without feeling scared or stupid about it.

Lyle bought some rabbits when he was out of high school. He was hoping to earn some extra money by selling rabbit fur. He built some rabbit coops for them out back by our garage. He started off with three pair of white angora rabbits. Before long, there were baby rabbits. They were really cute. Lyle was so busy with his job and other chores, that he asked me if I'd like to earn some money.

Well, I was always interested in earning money especially as my allowance was only twenty-five cents a week. Lyle offered to pay me a dime a day if I watered and fed the rabbits in the morning and again in the evening. This didn't seem to bad a deal to me.

The problem was in the winter. The weather was often below freezing. The rabbit's water would freeze I would have to go out with hot water and try to get it warm enough to knock the ice out of the tin can so that I could fill it up with fresh water. The rabbits didn't always cooperate and often tipped it out before I could fasten the wire again to the cage. When it got very cold, the rabbit pellets also stuck together and really made a mess of things. I also had to clean out their little huts. To keep warm in the winter, Lyle had built them a little hut inside their wire coops. When a pair of rabbits huddled in there all day, they also made their mess in there. I would have it lined with straw, but it all had to be cleaned out at least several times a week.

In the summer, it was much easier to take care of the rabbits. Sometimes I would let them out of their coops and make a wire cage down on the grass and let them eat the fresh grass. When they were little I could hold them much like I held my kittens. The older rabbits, especially the buck, was not very happy to be held though.

My mother also helped Lyle out, as she would clip their angora fur. I sometimes would help her hold them. Then the fur was weighed on our meat scale and then packaged up and sent to a company that would use them for angora mittens. I never knew how much Lyle made with his rabbits, but I was happy earning my dime a week.

After Lyle graduated from high school he became very sick. We found out that he had rheumatic fever. There was no other known cure except complete bed rest. Lyle had to stay up in his bedroom for much of that winter.

Some of his friends would come and play checkers or cards with him. He sometimes read books or magazines. He listened to the radio. We didn't have a television yet.

Lyle gradually felt better. The doctor told him it would be better for him to move to a dry warmer climate than Wisconsin. Lyle was only eighteen years old at this time. He wasn't ready to move away from his family yet, but the idea was planted.

Also, some of his friends were now signing up for the Army. However, because of his rheumatic fever the Army didn't want him. He was classified 4-F. He always felt bad about that. Lyle loved to play softball, and even though he couldn't play like he could in high school, he still played some ball. He would love to pitch and I was his catcher. He also tried to teach me to hit the ball.

Another idea Lyle had was to turn our hay field into a ball field. Usually my dad had a neighboring farmer cut the hay for his cows. Lyle figured that after the farmer cut it in the spring we could keep it cut with the lawn mower. Again, he offered to pay me for this project. If I would keep the ball field cut so that he could play ball out there with his friends, he would pay me a dollar. Wow, a whole dollar.

It took me three to four hours to cut the entire field. We had an old power mower that I had to push and push. But again, I would do anything to earn some money.

I also was happy to have an excuse to be outside. I loved being outside in the summer and feeling the warm sun. I could get a suntan just like my older sisters. But it seemed more fun doing it cutting the field, than just lying out on the roof of the house.

I was about nine years old when Lyle was working at the local cheese factory. He wanted to buy his own car. He had a car, but coming down the church hill on his way home from work one day, a parent picking up his child at my dad's school backed out into the road right into Lyle's car. It was smashed up pretty bad and so it had to be junked.

So, one afternoon after school I got to go along with Lyle and my dad to the neighboring small town to look for another used car. My dad had bought our 1946 Chevy there and so knew the owner of the car dealership. He had a used 1936 Chevy. As this was still in the early 1950's and not that far away from

World War II, cars from the 1930's were still around. Lyle was told he could take it out for a test drive.

I climbed into the back seat. My dad was in the front seat with Lyle. Lyle drove out of town onto the highway. All of a sudden, he hit a patch of ice. He put on the brake. Oops, there were no brakes. The car just started swerving and before we knew what was happening we were on the other side of the road. The spare tire was in the back seat with me. It rolled over me and then as we came to a stop it stopped rolling. Lyle and my dad crawled out of the front window and I followed them. Luckily, none of us were seriously injured except for a few bumps and bruises. We weren't very far from town and walked back to town. Someone saw us and gave us a ride back to the car dealer's.

Needless to say, Lyle didn't buy that car. We thought it would be better not to tell our mother as she would be upset. She didn't hear about the accident until many years later. I don't remember what car Lyle did buy.

After Lyle married and was working at a paper mill the opportunity came to him to work for a small printing firm in Arizona. Lyle drove out to Arizona to see what it was all about.

He came back quite excited about it. Marlene's parents had recently died so she was ready to make a fresh start. They were expecting their third child. Their new house was put on the market. As U-Haul wasn't in business yet at this time, Lyle arranged to buy a truck so that he could haul their home furnishings out to Arizona. Marlene would fly out with their two young daughters.

My family and Lyle's friends all helped Lyle and Marlene get ready for that big move. The move to the drier desert climate was good for his rheumatic fever. I didn't realize how much I would miss him and his young family.

They moved in the spring of my junior year in high school.

That first winter it was decided that my mother, younger brother and myself would go out to spend the Christmas holidays with them. It all was very exciting to plan. We could go out by train across almost the entire United States. My dad couldn't go because he had to play the church organ every Sunday and conduct the children's Christmas program and other special music for the holiday season.

As a big Wisconsin snow storm was predicted for the day we were planning to leave, my dad drove my mother, brother and myself over to my older sister's house. She lived in a small town where the roads were less likely not to be snowed in. We couldn't take any chances of being snowed in. It was a good thing we did that. That evening it snowed over ten inches. Fortunately, we arrived at the train station without too much trouble.

We would be taking the train from Appleton to Chicago. It was the Great Northwestern that ran once-a-day between Appleton and Chicago.

In a few years it would be the train that would take me back and forth to college.

In Chicago we had to change trains. We were riding the Great Northern and Santa Fe railroad. We would be riding coach as we couldn't afford to get the sleeping cars. It was four hours by train from Appleton to Chicago. That afternoon in Chicago we got on the train and rode all night sleeping in our seats. We had packed plenty of food to eat along the way. I brought magazines and books along to read. We played card games together. Also, I had just learned how to knit and was knitting myself a bright pink sweater. It was so thrilling to watch the countryside pass by our window.

A few places the train stopped long enough for us to get off and look around the train station. But generally we stayed on the train for the entire two days. In all it was about 48 hours from Chicago to Phoenix.

That year for Christmas my mother bought me a new Samsonite train case. She gave it to me early so that I could have it on the train. It was so neat. It had a number of small compartments in it where I could put all my special makeup, toothbrush and hairpins. I felt so grownup.

I was missing four days of high school so that we could get to Arizona in time for Christmas. But, because of the big snow storm that came in just as we were leaving, school was closed for three of those days.

It was exciting to see Arizona. Tall sequoia cactus were everywhere. Orange trees and lemon trees were in big fields. Date palms were also everywhere. Mesa was a small city at this time, about 22,000 in population, so there were still many fruit orchards in the valley.

Lyle and Marlene had just bought a small house. Their third child, a son had been born a few months earlier. He was so cute. I had lots of fun playing with him and his two older sisters.

Lyle showed us all around Mesa and the neighboring countryside. He took us on a road that was called the Apache Trail. It was a gravel road that was used in the late 1920's to build the Roosevelt Dam. It followed an old Indian trail. It was exciting going around and up and over the hills looking down into the valley.

One day we drove down to Mexico. I had been to Canada when my family visited our cousins in Niagara Falls but I had never dreamed of having the chance to go to Mexico. We only drove to a border town. It was eye opening for me to see the small houses that the Mexicans lived in. There were donkeys on the street and we could have a ride. Ponchos and piñatas were for sale. Brightly painted pottery was also sold out on the street. Everyone seemed so friendly. I didn't buy anything on this first visit, but I hoped that someday I would get a chance to visit again and stay longer.

A special trip to California was planned for over the New Year's. Marlene had a sister who lived near Disneyland. It was the first trip for our family to California. My dad had two brothers who lived there and we hoped to get to visit them also. They had moved to California in the late 1920's. I had met only one of them when he and his family had visited us in Wisconsin.

It was an eight-hour drive from Phoenix to southern California. There were eight of us to fit in Lyle's car. Somehow we managed with having the little ones sit on laps. We left after Lyle was finished working in his printing shop for the day. We took sandwiches and drinks with us in the car.

As we got closer to Los Angeles it was past midnight. It became very foggy. The others had all fallen asleep. I sat next to Lyle to keep him company. As the fog drew heavier Lyle had to put his head out of his window. I helped him by watching the middle white line. We traveled that way for over an hour. Soon we got to Marlene's sister's house in Anaheim.

It was fun to see how they celebrated Christmas without snow. There were lots of Santa's on the rooftops and lots of colored lights. I decided it was easier to decorate in the warmer weather.

Our first day there we went to Disneyland. It was great fun. There was so much to see. There were lots of rides and special exhibits. We went into the area called, The Old West. You could ride on a donkey. As we had purchased an all-day pass we could do as many things as we had time for. We talked Mother into riding on the donkeys also. It was fun to see our mother riding and having a good time. The day went by very quickly. It was better than the county fair.

The next day we toured Hollywood and looked at houses of famous movie stars. We also went to visit our other relatives. At my Uncle John's house they served us lunch. I remember tasting avocado salad for the first time. I thought it was Jell-O. I took a big mound of it on my plate. I tasted it. Yuck! What was this stuff? I was so embarrassed. I had never even seen a real avocado. My uncle had a tree in his backyard. I was getting more and more new experiences.

The highlight of California was going to the Rose Bowl Parade. We got up early in the morning so that we could get seats out front. We brought along some blankets to sit on. I bought a roll of color film. It was so exciting to see all the floats go by. It was much better than watching it on television. The parade lasted for several hours. We drove over to see where the Rose Bowl game was played, but we didn't have the money to buy tickets for the game.

Later that day we went to visit the other uncle and his wife who also lived in California. This was the only time I ever met them. I had heard he was a very good pianist and organist. His name was Marcus. Today my son Marcus is also a very good pianist and organist. I think there is something special in the name.

Before long it was time to leave California and then Arizona. The night we were to get on the train there was another big snowstorm in the Midwest. We sat up and played cards calling the train station every hour to find out when it would arrive. Finally about 3 AM we got word that it was due in around 4 AM. Lyle took us to the train station. It was hard to say goodbye.

Lyle and his family drove back to Wisconsin every other summer for many years. I was in college the next time I visited them in Arizona; I drove out with my sister and her husband, along with my mother and younger brother.

My parents were planning to move out to Arizona after my dad retired. But plans changed. My dad had a heart attack. Within two years he was diagnosed with bone cancer and he died within the year.

My mother decided to move out to Arizona on her own and would live near my brother and his family. I was happy when I got the chance to visit out West, but with his move it changed our family forever as we were no longer living in one small area of Wisconsin. Now there were thousands of miles between us.

My world had changed.

MOLASSES COOKIE MEN

4 cups sifted flour
1 teaspoon salt
1 teaspoon baking soda
2 teaspoons baking powder
2 teaspoons ginger
1 teaspoon cloves
1 teaspoon cinnamon
1 teaspoon nutmeg
1 cup sugar
1 cup shortening
1 cup molasses
2 eggs, separated

Sift flour with salt, baking soda, baking powder, and spices.
Cream shortening; add sugar gradually and beat until fluffy.
Add molasses and egg yolks.
Reserve egg whites for frosting
Mix well.
Thoroughly mix in flour mixture.
Wrap dough in waxed paper and chill until dough can be easily handled (at least 2 to 3 hours).
Roll out small portions of dough about 1/4 inch thick on lightly floured board, or pastry cloth.
Cut with an 8-inch gingerbread man cutter, or other Christmas or other holiday cookie cutters.
Place on ungreased baking sheet
Bake in 350-degree oven about 10 to twelve minutes.
Remove from oven.
Cool about two minutes before removing from baking sheet.
Cool completely and then frost and decorate as desired.

FROSTING

2 egg whites
3 cups sifted confectioners' sugar
Blend egg whites with sugar until frosting is proper consistency to go through decorating tube and hold shape.
Color with food coloring if desired.

Christmas tradition.

CHRISTMAS IN WISCONSIN

The highlight of Christmas for our family was the Christmas Eve service in church. My dad was in charge. We practiced and practiced our songs to sing. We practiced over and over again the special poems and Bible verses that we would recite in front of the entire congregation on Christmas Eve. Every student in the school had a Bible verse or religious Christmas poem to recite. Each grade a song to sing. Often two or three of the girls or boys got to sing a duet or trio. Sometimes, if you had a nice singing voice, you got to sing a solo.

While I liked to sing, I wasn't very good in doing harmony. I usually sang soprano. My favorite song was "O Holy Night," even though the range of notes stretched my soprano voice. It was from a German Christmas songbook that had been translated by A. T. Hanser in 1918. The seventh grade girls sang the song together and the song having three verses, we each were able to have a solo part.

Verse 1: O holy night, when from the realms of glory
Fair angels wing their gladdened flight to earth.
O holy night, when heaven's sweetest story,
Told to man of Jesus' wondrous birth.

Solo: Where trembling shepherds to their
Browsing flocks were tending,
Angelic hosts proclaimed, in myriad
Throngs descending.

Unison: Glory to God, glory to God,
Glory to God in the highest!

Verse 2: O holy Child, to whom with souls elated
Glad shepherds came to kneel before Thy throne.
O holy Child, for thee their hearts had waited,
Sweet Virgin's Child, God's beloved Son.

Solo: O, how their radiant eyes with heaven's
Light were gleaming!
O, how their happy songs from laughing
Lips were streaming!

Unison: Glory to God, glory to God,
Glory to God in the highest!

Verse 3: O holy night, so may Thy love and glory
Wring from each heart love's endless, happy lay!
O holy Child, and may Thy blessed story
Be proclaimed till time shall pass away,

Solo: And may each happy heart then,
Bathed in love light's splendor,
Repeat with solemn joy the angel song so tender.

Unison: Glory to God, glory to God,
Glory to God in the highest!

All the girls wore a new dress for this service. The boys wore a new shirt or tie. My mother always sewed a new dress for me to wear at the Christmas Eve service. We went into Appleton about a month before Christmas to do the shopping. We chose a pattern from the big pattern books in the back of the department store. "Simplicity," "Butterick" and "McCall's" were the pattern books we studied.

After we looked at all the patterns together, my mother allowed me to pick the one I liked best. She was a very good seamstress so I knew she could make any dress in the book. After we chose the pattern we would ask the clerk to find it in the correct size in the big pattern drawer. Then we looked at the fabric. There were rows and rows of different kinds of materials. One year I chose corduroy, another year a pretty wool plaid, and one year my grandma bought me some soft dark red velvet for a dress. On the back of the pattern package it would tell you how many yards of fabric you had to buy and what kind of zipper or other notions you needed to purchase.

After the fabric was picked out and measured by the clerk, we would pick out the buttons, zipper and thread. Sometimes the dress needed a hook and eye. I knew my mother could make it look just like it was in the pattern book.

My mother was very busy cutting out our dresses and fitting us. Both of my sisters also had a new dress sewn for them. When I was in sixth grade the princess line was in vogue. I got white corduroy with a dropped waist and then a full skirt. For seventh grade I had a plaid jumper with a lacy white blouse bought from a store. I felt that was a real treat.

In the eighth grade I begged and begged for a ready-made dress bought from a store. I had never had one. All the other girls had store bought dresses. Finally she gave in to my whining.

It was a big day when we went shopping for my dress. I couldn't find anything I liked, or that fit me just right. I finally settled on a shiny blue/gray striped dress with a dropped waist. It was okay, but not as pretty or well-fitting as the dresses my mother sewed for me.

I usually got a new pair of shoes for Christmas too. And sometimes my mother bought me a matching purse. We also went shopping for a new winter hat and gloves. This would be my church outfit for the rest of the winter and until the following Christmas. It was something I always looked forward too.

Before Christmas came I would have to try my dress on over and over again so that it would fit just right. Sometimes I tried it on when I came home at noontime for lunch. Or I would try it on right after school. If my mother had time she would sew a new dress for herself. My mother continued making her own clothing for the rest of her life. I can still hear her saying when she got a compliment on it, "Oh, I made this one, does it look all right?"

Before church on Christmas Eve everyone was excited. We would eat dinner early so that my dad could hurry to church. He would walk the quarter of mile, so that we could ride in the car. All the school children were to meet in the church basement a half hour before church. We all walked in together like a choir, two by two singing the first song with the choir. "O come all ye faithful" and "Tune your harps to gladdest songs Christians far and near" were the two favorite entrance hymns.

The school children all had to sit in front of the congregation. The first, second and third graders sat in the first two pews on the right. The fourth, fifth, sixth, seventh and eighth graders got to sit in the chairs that were set out for them in front of the first two pews. My dad could watch all this from the organ upstairs in the balcony with his mirror. We had practiced exactly where to sit. The minister was also sitting up front by the altar and he could also watch us. All the Children knew that their parents were watching them to, so we all sat still.

We sang our songs class by class, and recited our pieces one by one. The choir also sang some anthems and the congregation sang a few of their favorite carols. The pastor had a short sermon for this one evening.

First graders often had a recitation with hand motions.

Dear Jesus, we give our HEARTS to You.
Dear Jesus, we give our HANDS to You.
Dear Jesus, we give our VOICES to You.
Dear Jesus, we give our TIME to You.
Dear Jesus, we give our MONEY to You.
Dear Jesus, we give OURSELVES to You.

The students were all happy after all the recitations, solos and duets were over. Then came the best part. Each school child received a gift. My dad came downstairs and he would call out the name of each student, youngest to oldest to come forward and receive his/her gift. The gifts were usually a book, or a three-dimensional Christmas scene, a little bell, a pen, or maybe a miniature Bible.

The preschoolers who were seated with their parents in the congregation were also called up. First my dad called on the children he knew. Then he asked if there were any children he had missed. Often there were guests that in the church for Christmas Eve. They usually received a Bible coloring book, or a toddler Bible puzzle.

The church was always full, no matter what the weather was like. The church held about 250 people. It was usually very cold in Wisconsin in December and often there was snow on the ground.

The school children walked out to a happy hymn like "Joy to the world," or "Oh how joyfully, oh how merrily." When we got to the church entrance hall, we were given a big brown lunch bag. It was filled with peanuts, an orange and an apple and a smaller inside bag which was filled with hard candy and rock candy. Rock candy was a hard caramel covered with a thin layer of chocolate. It was a hard crunch and then it dissolved in your mouth. It tasted wonderful.

Everyone quickly put on their coats and hurried to the car for the quick drive home. Even though we knew it was my mother who put the gifts under the tree, we pretended that Santa had arrived while we were in church. My Dad, by this time, was quite exhausted and preferred to go to his study to unwind. It was as if the church was his Christmas celebration and at home was my Mother's.

My dad usually bought us a gift and gave it to us unwrapped. It was usually a book. However, the Christmas before I started college he bought me a new portable Smith Corona typewriter. I would type a lot of papers with it, and also earn money because I often typed papers for other students at college.

The year I was in third grade I begged and begged for the complete set of the *Bobbsey Twin* books. I had seen them advertised in the big Sears Christmas catalog. I loved to read the *Bobbsey Twins*. Our school library had quite a few of their books, but this would be my very own set. I got a big box for Christmas. It looked like the box of books. But when I opened up the box, there were books, but not the Bobbsey Twin set. There was *Treasure Island, Huckleberry Finn, Tom Sawyer, Heidi* and two *Bobbsey Twins* books!

I was so disappointed. I hadn't heard of most of the other stories. I knew I should be thankful for all these books. There were thirty books in all. I couldn't hide my dismay. It would take me a number of years to appreciate these wonderful classics and to realize the world my dad was trying to open for me.

My mother's gifts were wrapped and laid under the tree.

The Christmas I remember the most was when I got my big doll Julie. I had wanted this doll so badly. I had seen her in the big Sears Roebuck Christmas catalog. She could say Mama when she was tipped from front to back. She had lovely auburn hair, a cloth body, and arms and legs that felt real. Her face had such a pretty smile.

Julie was the picture of a little girl of two or three. She was twenty-six inches tall. I was six at the time and this would be my last doll. Age has taken its toll on her, but I still have her. Her arms and legs are bandaged as the rubber has worn out, but the cloth body is still good and she can still say Mama these 50 years later.

An earlier Christmas I got my doll house. This gift actually came before Christmas.

I begged and begged for Christmas to hurry up and come. It was a snowy Sunday afternoon before Christmas and everyone was busy. Finally, my Mother brought down the doll house. I was enraptured. I set the furniture up in the style the pamphlet showed. I was afraid to do it any other way. I even had people: a mother, father, sister and brother. Later on, I got more people and the family grew.

I played many rainy and snowy afternoons in my own world that I created with my families. Their house was always tidy. The children always behaved. The parents didn't yell at each other. It was my fantasy world.

I still have it. Some of the plastic furniture has been broken. I have let my own children, and also some of the classes I have taught, play with it. It is so interesting to listen to the children create their world of make-believe, which often sounded so real.

As I grew older, and toys became a thing of the past, I received clothes for Christmas. Boots, ice skates, and games such as Cootie, Uncle Wiggley, and Monopoly were also welcomed gifts. But Julie, the doll and the doll house remained especially sweet in my memories.

My dad didn't want his children to believe in Santa Claus. I knew of him from the other Children in school and from books. The year I was five he gave me a special pop-up book about Santa and his helpers. At the end of the story it talked about Jesus giving gifts and ends with the carol, "Silent Night."

I was so excited! The year I was six I was allowed to go to Fremont to see Santa Claus. Fremont was a small town about seven miles from our house. I knew Santa wasn't real, but we were allowed to pretend with my younger brother. Loren went with me. Maybe my older siblings convinced my parents there was no harm in letting my younger brother believe in Santa and to let us see him.

Santa Claus was coming to the big fire hall. There were over 100 children there. Everyone was excited. First there was a movie. Then the firemen blew the whistle to announce Santa Claus was coming. He had a bag of candy to give to each child. The fireman also passed out a coloring book and a box of crayons. I don't remember sitting on Santa's lap, or telling him what I wanted. Maybe that was only for the real little Children. But it was fun getting the candy, and pretending that there really was a Santa Claus who brought you presents.

It was hard for my mother living out in rural Wisconsin. She felt stuck out in the country. She wanted to bring some city-like class to our home. Even though she had grown up in rural Wisconsin, the home we were living in was not as modern as the house she had lived in twenty years earlier with her parents. Country living, without modern conveniences was not easy.

She was always looking in magazines and trying to make our decorations to be like those in the magazines. We put snow on the windows, using stencils. One time, my sister LeAnne, and I painted a branch and hung angel hair in a wispy fashion around it.

Grandma Hoewisch, one of the oldest church members had a real Christmas tree and decorated it with real candles. It was a beautiful sight to behold! Everyone would be called in to watch the lighting of the candles. Then my dad would lead us all in singing some carols. The tree was freshly being cut earlier that week from the nearby woods. I stared at the tree never having seen anything quite so beautiful.

Our tree was usually bought in the small village about three miles from our house. It cost two dollars. My mother tried to stay modern and often did exotic things with the tree. One year she sprayed it gold, another year silver. One year she put all blue ornaments on the tree and another year all red ornaments.

Cookie baking was a big part of the season. That usually began three or four weeks ahead of time. Gingerbread boys, angels and other form cookies were the main ones my mother baked. They all had to be frosted one by one with different colored icing. Then sprinkles and silver balls were carefully sprinkled on the cookies. The silver balls were so hard you could easily chip a tooth if you tried to bite one rather than suck it.

By the time I was eleven I often frosted the cookies when my parents went to the church Christmas party. The Ladies Aid and the Men's Club met jointly for the party. They played games and sometimes showed a movie. Then they gave each other gifts.

Then they enjoyed eating special food for Christmas time.

I looked forward to the night when they had their Christmas party, because that was the night I would frost the Christmas cookies. I sometimes got my younger brother Loren to help me, but he often got too sloppy and messy, so I would usually finish the cookies by myself.

The Ladies Aid met on Thursday afternoons and the Men's Club met on Thursday evenings. Before I went to school I had to go with my mother to the meetings. They were very boring for a little girl. All the women did was talk. Sometimes they had a guest come in and speak to them. They talked about raising money for church work, like missionaries who went overseas. After all the talking the women had desert and coffee. I got some too. I never went to the Men's Club meeting. I suppose they talked like the women did and then had their food. My dad was the secretary and wrote down what they talked about.

One year I tried to make a Gingerbread House. It was a lot of work and took a lot of frosting. When I was all done, it was crooked. We saved it until Christmas to eat, but the frosting became very hard.

Before I close on my cookie baking, I must tell of Grandma Hoewisch. My cookie baking was fun, and decorating a task that I enjoyed, but for her cookie decorating was an art. She decorated the angels with icing as thin as tinsel using a toothpick to outline the faces. Her churches looked like a Currier and Ives print. It was hard to think of eating such a cookie. Often we saved her cookies for months. They were so beautiful! By the time we ate them though, they were often so hard they didn't taste good anymore.

Another Christmas event that was important especially as I grew older was caroling to the older members of our church and neighborhood. The choir carpooled on the Sunday before Christmas or an evening near the holiday. "Silent Night," was sung both in English and German. To see tears swelled up in the eyes of the older members brought an awareness and a meaning to Christmas that extended beyond anything that I had every realized before.

I learned as I grew older that Christmas could be special in a quiet kind of way by going to church, singing in the choir, family dinner, or visiting other parishioners. In the days following we drove over to my aunts and uncles homes. Gifts were not exchanged, but goodwill was and hymn singing, games and good food were in abundance.

Christmas was full of memories, family, tradition, the birth of our Savior, and peace on earth. We can have peace on the earth. Why do nations quarrel and go to war? Are we not all in God's universe? Will the world ever resolve their conflicts and accept peace on earth, goodwill to men?

CHRISTMAS STOLLEN

4 lbs. flour (16 cups)
1/4 lb. almonds (if desired)
1/2 lb. butter (1 cup)
Rind of one lemon
1 quart milk (scaled)
2 teaspoon. salt
1/2 teaspoon nutmeg
6 eggs
1 lb. raisins
1 lb. currants
1 1/2 cup sugar
2 cakes yeast

Cream sugar and butter.
Dissolve yeast, add to milk
Add eggs.
Sift dry ingredients and alternating add flour and liquid.
Add fruits and nuts.
Let raise 3 hours, knead and raise another hour or so in pans.
Bake 375 degrees for 25 minutes.
Makes two loaves and 2 round (half recipe.)

Frost with powdered sugar icing when cool.

½ lb. powdered sugar
1 teaspoon vanilla
2 Tablespoons butter
Milk (Just enough for creamy consistency)

Make smaller loaves for gift giving.

SUMMERS IN THE WINDY CITY

Berry picking was a good job for a young girl in rural Wisconsin. I enjoyed being out in the fresh air day after day. It was fun being with your friends out in the fields. It was hard work though, and the pay wasn't all that great.

In the seven summers I worked there I was paid the same as the day I started. I was their fastest picker, but weather conditions also were a big factor in how much money I could make. There were several summers when the berries weren't all that good either because of too much or too little rain.

I wanted to get a regular job in the nearby city taking care of children. My sister had been able to get a job down in a Chicago suburb, but until I was sixteen, I knew my parents wouldn't let me go to Chicago.

Then I saw an ad in our local paper placed by a couple in a nearby well-to-do community looking for a young girl to take care of their two children. I answered the ad right away, and before long I was asked to come and meet the parents. My parents drove me into town.

After meeting the parents and learning what all the responsibilities would be, it was decided that I could start working there as soon as school was out. I was ecstatic. The pay would be twenty dollars a week. I could board there, and get one day off a week. I was basically babysitting the children to give the mother free time. Twenty dollars a week seemed like an awful lot of money to me. For the summer I could earn two hundred dollars. In berry picking I was happy if I made one hundred dollars and I thought this would be a lot less work.

As it turns out, the week before I was to start my job, my mother got a telephone call from the woman. The young lady that had worked for them the summer before had asked for her job back. She had hoped to get a job in Chicago, but it had fallen through. They had really liked her, and as the children knew her already, the mother was sorry, but said they hoped I understood.

I was deeply disappointed. I had hoped to explore the twin cities of Neenah and Menasha. I was going to be living in the city. Now it was back to berry picking for another summer. My mother said, "Someday soon, you too birdie can fly away." It seemed a long way off at the time.

The next spring I started watching for ads in the Appleton paper that we received through the mail. It was always a day late as they didn't have carrier service out where we lived. Usually reading the paper didn't matter to me. I could hear all the important headlines in the evening television news.

And then one night there was a three line ad from a family in suburban Wilmette, Illinois, a northern suburb of Chicago. She gave her address and asked for a letter with references. I worked and worked on my letter and had it sent off within a week. The Guidance Counselor at the high school offered to write me a letter of recommendation. Did I have a chance? I had no idea. I just knew I wanted a job down by Chicago. I wanted to see the world. My dad talked a lot about Chicago. He had taken summer school courses down there at the Lutheran Teacher's College. He had gone there as far back as the 1930's for the World's Fair. Chicago was filled with museums, theaters and Riverview, a big amusement park.

Within a few weeks I got an answer back from Mrs. Stahl. She was very pleased with my letter and references. She told me a little about the family. They had four children, ages three to ten. I would have one day off a week. During the week I was to supervise the children, take them to the park and the beach. I would have to help serve their meals, and supervise their bedtime.

It was like babysitting, only more of it. I would be allowed to go to church on Sundays.

She mentioned also that I would have a room of my own. On my day off I sometimes could have use of the family car. I was so excited. She was offering me the job. The pay was twenty-five dollars a week. What with getting room and board it sounded like a lot of money to me.

They wanted me to start as soon as school was out. That would leave me no time for any other time off or vacation. My adventures were beginning.

My parents drove me down to Wilmette. It was a four-hour drive. I packed shorts, slacks, my Sunday dresses, some books to read, curlers, sneakers and rubber soled sandals or flip flops as we liked to call them. They made a flip-flop sound as I walked with them.

We arrived at the Stahl's in the early afternoon. She served ice tea. We never had ice tea before. Everything appeared so sophisticated. My dad could talk to anyone, so conversation was not a problem. I just sat and listened. My dad assured her that I was a good worker and that she could expect to get full value from me. She was to let him know if there were any problems.

Then I got to meet the children. They were adorable, especially little Amy. She was just three years old and a little doll. Then there were Tommy and Peter, five and six years old. They looked like typical little boys. Some mischief in their eyes, but they were both very polite. The oldest child was Nancy a young girl of ten. She seemed very grown up.

In a few minutes my parents left. I was here on my own in Wilmette, sixteen years old.

That evening Mr. Stahl came home from the office. He seemed like a nice man, dark hair and very good looking. I didn't know what to say to him. He didn't appear at all like the farmers that I was used to back in Wisconsin. He was more like the principal at the high school. He was very polite, but formal.

Mrs. Stahl went over the guidelines with me. She told me that she expected the children to listen to me and that I must remember that I am the grown up and should know what to do. I was not to let the children tell me what to do.

The children would be expected to pick up their rooms, clear off their own dinner settings, and generally follow the rules.

There were a lot of other children in the neighborhood and also more Mother's Helpers as we were known. The children would take turns going to each other's houses. I was to make sure I always knew where all four children were and what they were doing.

The first week Mrs. Stahl went with us to the beach. It was about three miles from their house. Lake Michigan had beautiful sandy beaches. Some days the water was calm as can be, and other days the waves made swimming almost impossible.

Mrs. Stahl wanted her children to play outside as much as possible. We could go to the beach every day the weather permitted. I couldn't believe it. I loved going to the beach. I laid on the blanket and watched the children play. I went in the water and played with the children. Before long, I had a deep dark suntan. This was long before I had heard about skin cancer. I loved lying out on the sand and feeling the warm sun on my skin.

I took the children to the beach almost every day. We would come home for lunch, usually peanut butter and jelly sandwiches, and then everyone was to lie down for an hour.

Amy usually took a nap, and the boys were expected to be quiet. Nancy was allowed to be reading in bed. This was my time to clean up the kitchen and tidy up the house a bit.

Once a week, Mrs. Stahl had a housekeeper come in to do the major cleaning. She was an African-American woman. This was the first time I really ever met a black person. She was very friendly. Sometimes she brought along her young granddaughter to play with Amy. She also helped with the ironing. This was before the days of wash and wear, so all the children's shorts and tops needed ironing. I helped with the laundry and sometimes helped with the ironing as I could do this in the evenings after the children had gone to bed.

After the children's rest time, we usually stayed around the neighborhood. On particularly hot days, we would go back to the beach for the afternoon.

A few times, we went to the Country Club to swim in the pool. The Stahls didn't belong, but Mr. Stahl's parents did and so they could visit it on their membership. A few times we went shopping together in the local stores for children's clothing.

Mrs. Stahl really liked being able to go to the grocery story by herself. In the winter she always had to take the two youngest children along. Sometimes she went shopping, or played golf or tennis with her friends.

Mrs. Stahl planned the evening meal. I usually ate with the children, while Mrs. Stahl waited for Mr. Stahl to come home from the office and they had dinner by themselves.

I took the children upstairs to read them stories and get them ready for bed. After they were in bed, I could have the rest of the evening to myself if the Stahl's were staying in.

Sometimes I went to visit another Mother's Helper. A few times I could have the family car and I would pick up several of the girls and we would go to the movies. One night, we went to a new theater and I took a wrong turn. I was afraid I wouldn't be able to find my way back. We stopped for gas and asked directions. Fortunately, we weren't too far out of our way, but it reminded me to be very careful and watch the street signs better.

Monday was my day off, as it was for most of the Mother's Helpers. We often went in to downtown Chicago to go shopping. I had bought a guide to Chicago to learn about all the special museums and other sights. I wanted to use my time off to really get to know the city.

Most of the museums were free and usually one or two of the girls would go with me.

Some of the girls wanted to use this time to go to the beach or a movie. I liked movies, but tried to see them on the week nights when I got the evening off. I particularly wanted to see a stage play.

The first play I saw was *West Side Story*. The dancing, the music, and the story held me in rapture. I could go again and again. I thought the city was the most wonderful place to be.

My dad had often talked about Riverview Park. It was a big amusement park built back in the 1930's. He told about the ride where you were spun around and then the floor was taken away. He talked about the giant roller coaster. It sounded like to so much fun.

It was like a giant county fair. As it was quite a distance from where the Stahl's lived, Mr. Stahl agreed to take us there one morning on his way to work. There were four of us girls.

The neighborhood where it was located was not so good anymore. I know Mr. Stahl was worried about us country girls in the big city, but we assured him we would be careful. We would stay together the entire day, and meet him at the entrance at five o'clock promptly.

We had a great time. We found the ride where centrifugal force took over. We went on the big Ferris Wheel. We did the Tilt-a-Whirl and the Loop-de-Loop. We walked through the crazy mirrors and ate cotton candy. It was a most wonderful day.

Another time I went with the Stahl's when they were going to visit Mr. Stahl's parents who owned a large home on Lake Michigan. It was a lovely estate. I was now getting more accustomed to this grander life style, but I was still in awe of it. Mr. Stahl called me into his father's study. There was a baseball game on. And what did I see, but green grass on the ball field. It was television in color. I had heard about color coming to television, but had yet to see it. It was so real. It was like being there. It was hard to believe that someday that most Americans would earn enough to buy their own color television set. It seemed unreal at this time.

I wrote my parents every week to let them know how I was doing. I saved most of my money as I knew it was needed for my school clothes. I bought some fabric to sew myself a few new blouses, shorts and dresses.

I was also expected to attend church every Sunday. Mrs. Stahl usually attended in the winter, but summer was her time off. But she knew my parents expected me to attend. Sometimes I took one or two of the children with me. I felt very grown up attending a church service all by myself in suburban Chicago.

Mrs. Stahl had many books in her house so I didn't lack for reading. We also took the children to the library and got story books for them and I checked out books on Mrs. Stahl's card. She had a bicycle I could ride and sometimes in the evening I just rode around the neighborhood.

Before long the summer was nearly over. I couldn't believe it. It seemed a long time ago that I had picked berries for the summer. And now the Stahl's were talking about spending a vacation in Wisconsin. I couldn't believe it. Why would they come to Wisconsin for a vacation? What was there to do in Wisconsin?

As it turned out, they rented a house on a lake not too far from my parents. Mrs. Stahl, the children and I came up on the train. Mr. Stahl and his brother drove the car pulling a boat. This was going to be a different vacation than I was used to. Mrs. Stahl's mother was also coming along. She lived in Connecticut and flew out.

The Stahl's rented a very big country house on the lake. The boat got put in at the dock. I had learned to water ski from my sister LeAnne and her husband Willard just the summer before. The Stahl's were happy to have me ski. It was so much fun. The big sport was to ski with one ski. I had never tried it. Here was my chance to really show off. Well, I was a bit too optimistic and as I threw off the one ski completely lost my balance and hit the water hard. Ouch, it hurt!

My feelings though were hurt more. I should have known better than to show off. They all thought that I had given it a good try. But from then on I stuck with two skis. That night my ear began to hurt. I often had ear aches as a young child. Ear aches were painful. Now, my ear was draining fluid.

Oh, what had I done?

I was afraid to let Mrs. Stahl know, I didn't want to spoil the vacation. I took aspirin and just let it drain. I had trouble with that ear from then on. I found out later that I had ruptured an ear drum, probably from hitting the water so hard. It could have been just from childhood ear aches, but I don't think so.

Many years later I was able to have it repaired and what a difference it made for water sports.

The two weeks on the lake flew by. It was time for the Stahl's to go back to Chicago and for me to go back home and finish my last year in high school.

I was able to work for the Stahl's for one more summer. It was another magical summer for me. I was able to find jobs for two of my good friends from high school. We visited with each other almost daily. We had our days off together. The Stahl's gave me a five dollar a week raise. But as I needed to earn even more money for college that year, Mr. Stahl agreed to let me do some typing for him. He was vice-president of a plastic firm and they were busy trying to get new clients. I typed up letters and addressed envelopes. I was paid an extra ten dollars a week for several evenings of work.

I had to do that in the evenings after the children were in bed. I set up the typewriter on the screened porch where there was a television. I thought, "What a lovely life?" I was getting paid, sitting outside, watching television, and all I had to do was type.

Towards the end of the summer Mrs. Stahl drove me over to see Concordia Teacher's College which was located in a western suburb of Chicago. I had been accepted as a student there earlier in the spring of my senior. I had decided to follow my father's footsteps and become a school teacher. Mrs. Stahl thought it was a lovely campus. It was smaller than I expected, but it was near the city and I knew a new life was starting for me.

On my eighteenth birthday, Mrs. Stahl bought me tickets to go to the outdoor theater to see *A Raisin in the Sun*, the play by Lorraine Hansbury. It was a most touching play that furthered my education in learning about the world and all the different cultures. My little world of rural Wisconsin was opening up.

The Stahl's took another two-week vacation to Wisconsin. I was only able to stay with them one week as I had many things to do to prepare for college. The Stahl's and I stayed in touch for many years.

HEAVENLY SPAGHETTI

1 pkg. (7 oz) spaghetti
1 Tablespoon butter
1 1/2 lbs. ground round
8 oz. sour cream
8 oz. cottage cheese
8 oz. cream cheese
8 oz. can tomato sauce
6 oz. can tomato paste
1 Tablespoon minced green pepper
1/2 cup chopped green onion
1 can of mushroom pieces (or fresh mushrooms sautéed first)
Salt & pepper to taste

Cook & drain spaghetti.
While spaghetti is cooking, sauté beef and mushrooms in butter until brown.
Add tomato paste and tomato sauce, salt and pepper.
Combine cheeses and sour cream with onions and green pepper.
Be sure to set out cream cheese a while before beginning recipe so it softens.
Layer spaghetti, cheese mixture and meat sauce.
Refrigerate overnight.
Bake at 350 degrees oven for twenty minutes covered and 35 minutes uncovered.

Serve with garlic bread, and French cut green beans, green tossed salad.

Easy company dinner.

WISCONSIN WINTER

The two words are almost synonymous to many people, cold and snow. I can remember asking my mother once if it rained in the winter and then quickly realized how foolish my question was as most certainly it was too cold to rain in the winter!

But for a child there were many winter pleasures.

Our house was at the bottom of two hills, the big church hill and the smaller school hill. Next to our house, across the driveway, was the field. A small field for a farmer, but big enough for a softball field in the summer and a wonderful ice rink in the winter.

The conditions had to be just right. First the field would have to be cut or mowed in the fall. Sometimes my dad burned it off, which I watched with great interest but not without some anxiety. The need was to keep the fire line on the other side of the driveway. My Mother always said, "Daddy's playing with fire!"

Hopefully then, we would get some early snow and maybe a late fall rain, then freezing and snow, melt again, and repeat. By Christmas the field would be flooded. January was when the deep cold set in and then the ice pond would be ready.

At night, Mother would turn on the porch light and I would take my skates and pretend I was some famous ice skater twirling around on the ice. Sometimes, a bunch of children would come over and we'd play games like Tag, or the Whip. The strongest skater would be first in line with the lightest kid on the end of the line. Everyone linked hands and we'd skate together faster and faster and then the leader would swing the line around and "Whee, crack the whip!" Without a tight grip, one went sailing off across the ice.

Parents didn't always approve of this game as the person on the end could easily fall if they weren't a sure skater. To a child it was exhilarating, and, except for the County Fair, one never got such a ride!

After an hour or two of skating I wound up with wet mittens, soaked snow pants, red cherry cheeks and I was ready to go into the house for a wonderful cup of hot chocolate.

Sometimes my dad allowed the school children to come down to the pond during noon recess. In later years, a few church members complained of that practice, saying that it wasn't proper education! Ironically, in later years, ice hockey became a high school sport. In the city, parents took children for ice skating lessons. In other schools ice skating was part of physical education. Our physical education program was as changeable as the seasons and as imaginative as the games we could think of to play. Girls and boys played together, long before co-ed games became mandated.

Snow was a major component of a Wisconsin winter. When the snow came too fast and heavy, ice-skating was out of the question. To shovel off a big field by hand was too awesome a task even for the most hardy souls. The farmers with plows would be too busy doing their own snow-plowing for their long driveways or roads to the barn to bother with the ice pond for the children. Occasionally a farmer plowed our driveway so that we didn't need to shovel it. But snow was good for many things. It provided an insulation for the earth for the long cold winter nights that were yet to come. The other wonderful advantage was that a snowstorm packed needed snow on the roads so that I could go sledding!

We never owned a toboggan, although in later years we would go over to the Hortonville hill and rent one for a Sunday afternoon of sledding fun down some really high and long hills.

With the right snow cover over the black top road by our house, and firm packing the church and school hills were ready for perfect sledding. The county worker hardly ever cleared the township roads down to the black top between November and March. The men would be too busy keeping the state roads open.

Usually I would sled with another friend so that we could watch together for cars, but sometimes, I would venture out by myself. I would look carefully into the distance, get a running head start, steer near the side of the road, listen for car engines, and enjoy!

If the snow was packed well, a slight breeze was blowing, my run was ambitious and with a little luck thrown in, I would make it to the school hill. Then with another hill for momentum I could almost make it home. Exhilarating is the only word to describe it. Crisp, cold, clean air and wind splashing against my face was all I could want.

But then of course, I had the long walk up the hill again. I would get all out of breath. And if I was out with my little brother, I had to give him a ride back up the hill on the sled. I would pant even more. But, oh, the ride down the hill was worth it!

In later years, the Zion School Board decided it was too dangerous for the school children to slide down the hill during recess school time, as Zion church would be responsible for any accidents. No one ever got hit by a car or hurt that I can remember.

Another activity on the ice rink was what my oldest brother called "practicing driving in an emergency." He took the car out on the ice rink and practiced driving students. My mother wasn't too thrilled about this, but didn't have a good argument against it as icy roads were a fact of life in Wisconsin. As an adult, my brother moved to Arizona, so he never got much use out of all his practicing!

Sometimes the snow came too fast and furious even for Wisconsin snowplows. Even for the Big Winnebago County plow. The Big Winnebago had not only the two big tall center blades over ten feet high, but each center blade had an extension blade so there was a total of four blades.

One snowstorm, the snow came so fast and was packed so tightly that the big county plow could not push the snow to clear a path on the road for the cars. Then a big Winnebago came by the other side of the road, past our house on the left, and was stuck.

We were snowbound. One particular big snow bank was blocking the road to the right of us, and another huge snow bank was blocking the road to the left of us. The two huge snow banks were about a mile apart.

School was cancelled. Hooray! And what to do? I called my friends over and together we went climbing on the snow banks!

The banks reached ten to fifteen feet, clear up to the telephone poles. Car antennas in the winter wore red ties, so that another driver could notice a car coming around a corner that had high snow banks. A bunch of children met out by the big bank, shovels were brought, and serious tunneling was done. We built a snow house, or hid in the snow bank, a true igloo. The stalemate lasted for only two days and the plows broke through the heavy snow at last. The excitement of creating a real snow house was never to be forgotten.

When school resumed, we were anxious to return to classes so that we could play all the winter sport games. Fox and Goose was a big favorite. A long, winding, complicated trail was tramped out in the ball field, zigzag, crossover, dead end circles, on and on the path went. Then the fox was chosen and he had to do the catching. Everyone else was a goose. The race was on. If one accidentally got cornered in a dead end, or went off the path and got noticed by the fox, that person became the fox. Or you became the fox if the fox tagged you. Then the old fox could rest and he became one of the geese.

Unless we played the mean way, the fox couldn't be tagged immediately back again. There had to be an intervening person who was the fox, otherwise one poor soul was it all recess, and the game really slowed down as they became more and more out of breath. Sometimes we built in safety spots where one could rest and not be tagged. Fox and Goose was a wonderful way to burn off excess energy.

We always went outside for recess. In later years, when I taught school in Vermont, I remember minus ten degrees Fahrenheit was the cut-off point to play outside during recess. In Wisconsin, before anyone had heard of the wind chill factor we bundled up in layer upon layer of heavy woolen clothes and went outside. Only Richard, my friend with asthma, was allowed to stay in. The real cold damp air was too hard on his lungs.

In high school, it was not in vogue to bundle up too much. This was long before neat looking snow boots, or smart ski pants. Winter clothes were bulky. Wool snow pants, which smelled as they were drying in front of the stove, knitted mittens that got soaked through to your skin, and heavy rubber boots that fit over your shoes were all part of my regular winter gear. All this clothing gave me the overall appearance of a wooly mammoth! And then for the final effect, a big woolen scarf wrapped around your neck two or three times. Boys wore caps with ear liners.

Wearing this kind of outfit on the bus, into the city for high school was definitely out if you didn't want to be the laughing stock of the city children. As a girl I felt compelled to wear impractical shoes, matching sweater sets, jacket and maybe a scarf around my neck, but not on my head. Little angora headbands became the rage and there were matching mittens to complete the outfit. This necessitated stepping carefully in somebody else's track out to the school bus, with the hope that upon returning home at night, a few tracks from the morning would still be there to get me back into the house without freezing or getting my feet too wet. Mother, of course, didn't approve of this apparel She didn't fuss too much about it though as she knew the importance to me of fitting in. That was very important to me. I didn't want to look like a country bumpkin.

Winter never seemed long and dreary. Maybe because I didn't know anything else. But I would rather think it was because I saw, felt, and experienced winter as fun. Ice and cold were all avenues to different activities that differed from summertime experiences. The contrast of first being out in the cold, and the welcome return to a warm cozy cook stove was exhilarating, even to me as a child.

Henry was three classes ahead of me. He was with Raymond, Billy and Kathy. Kathy and I were really good friends. She loved to draw and to talk. For the latter, she was always getting into trouble. She was called Kathy, the Chatterbox. Billy was nice, when no one was around, but sometimes he was a bully. Raymond was the menace. He was too big for his grade. He only came to our school for 7th and 8th grade and probably was 15 or 16 years old. Most of the children in the school came from 6 years of age on, and thus not too many new faces showed up. Raymond was big and because of that, he thought he should be the boss and especially tell us girls what to do. He thought that he should be boss more certainly than a Teacher's Kid should.

I wasn't about to put up with anything from Raymond. So, one day I had my chance to get even with him. He had let the air out of my bicycle tires one afternoon when he had received permission to go to the out house. I was so mad! That meant I had to walk my bike home, the very idea! The next time it was my turn to take the flag down, two minutes before the closing bell, instead of running in and being at my desk for the closing prayer I took my chances that my Dad wouldn't notice. I waited out by Raymond's bike. To let the air out of his tires didn't occur to me, he had a three mile ride home, and I did sort of liked him. I just didn't want him to bully me.

When he ran out of school to get on his bike I was there waiting for him. I reached out to him and took my long sharp fingernails and scratched him down the side of his arm. It drew blood and surprised him. Needless to say, he didn't bully me any longer and my tires were safe.

January 10th I always remember as Henry's birthday. I particularly remember the year he turned 14. I was 11.

Henry was cute and smart, but short. He never got past five feet five inches, so even in grade school I towered over him, as I did over all the children. I was five feet seven inches by the time I was in sixth grade. Except Raymond, he was taller than me. Henry liked Janice. She was short and had red hair that came down to her shoulders in locks.

Her mother carefully styled her locks by wrapping them up in rags each morning before school. Janice was very attractive and I was jealous. But Henry was fair. He invited all the children in the top four grades to his birthday party.

It was a Saturday afternoon. We were to bring our ice skates and we would go sledding on the Rat River. It was a beautiful river, frozen clear, ten to fourteen inches deep. I could see fish swimming underneath the ice and the ice creaked or crackled now and then. I think I was scared it might break through, although I knew his Dad wouldn't let us be there if it wasn't perfectly safe. The ice crackling was just nature's way of settling the ice, and at ten degrees below zero, it wasn't about to melt.

Henry's Dad brought us to the side of the road by the bridge where we were to skate. But there was one problem. It was very cold that day and it was windy. By the time my skates were on, my fingers were numb. There was no warming shed, or a fire or even a car for wind protection. And then I had to slide down the bank to the ice.

I remember being extremely cold! I skated around, and I don't know how long we stayed, but we played tag and other ice games, and then when we were finished skating, we had to get back up the riverbank. By now, all feeling had left my fingers. It was a struggle to take off my skates and get back into my shoes and boots. I just wanted to get my fingers warm.

When we got back to the house, Henry's Mom, seeing my very cold fingers, wouldn't let me put them under warm water. It had to be cold water. It was a new technique she had heard about. Then she rubbed my fingers in a towel and eventually feeling started coming back. To this day my fingers often give me pain and turn white as a sheet when they get cold. What hurt even more that day, was that the rest of the children went into the barn and played games up in the hayloft. I always suspected that I was left out on purpose, being the Teacher's Kid, but I'll never know.

Winter wasn't all fun for children in the country. There was wood to bring in from the wood pile, or coal to shovel in the furnace. Walks needed to be shoveled, and the school courtyard needed to be kept clean. Mittens were constantly being dried out next to the furnace pipes. For the mothers doing the laundry, before the day of clothes dryers, finding spaces to hang all the laundry became a real challenge. Hopefully, canned goods from the summer crops were ample as buying groceries was limited to once-a-week.

Many afternoons, after chores were done, we played board games. Monopoly was a favorite and the game could go on for weeks.

One night after dinner, when we children often fooled around, my oldest brother challenged me to do sit-ups. Well, they looked easy enough, I thought, "What's the big deal?" "Bet you can't do a 100," my brother said. "Bet I can," I replied.

My brother said he would give me a penny for each one I did, if I did 100. I could make a whole dollar. Wow! A whole dollar. I could certainly do that! I was off. I started quite fast, 1, 2, 3, 4, 5, 6, well, we'll see. I got to fifty without any difficulty, then up to 75. Oh, I knew I could do it. Then I gradually went slower. Well, he didn't say it had to be in five minutes. Wow, a dollar that was the same as three hours of babysitting money. It seemed a much easier way to earn a buck. I did it! Wow!

Everyone was impressed. Why the big deal? This was before the cult of bodybuilding and physical fitness that took over the country. Besides, I was in good shape. But, the next morning, I felt a twinge in my abdominal muscles.

What could it be? I sure didn't know. At school it got worse. It seemed as if I couldn't stand up straight. Oh my, what was the problem? And then I knew. Oh no. I was paying the price for doing the 100 sit-ups. Oh my, why didn't someone warn me? Would I ever be the same again? What was to become of me, what was this? Oh, I hurt so much. I don't remember getting any sympathy. It was once again, "Oh, Louise." The pain gradually went away of course. I had my dollar, and I showed everybody I could do it.

CARAMELS

1 cup white sugar
1 1/2 cup dark corn syrup
1/2 lb. butter
1 pint half and half
1 teaspoon. vanilla
Nuts (optional)

Mix sugar, syrup, butter and 1/2 pint of half and half.
Let it boil a half-hour.
Add the rest of the half and half slowly so that the candy will not stop boiling.
Let boil until it forms a soft-ball in cold water (1 hour plus)
Add vanilla.
Add nuts.
Put on half pecan per piece.
Wrap individually in plastic wrap.

Melts in your mouth.

LEAVING THE NEST

The week before I was to start my most far-reaching journey of my 18-year-old existence my mother decided to prepare me by taking me to the city beauty shop to get a permanent hair wave.

This was before blow dryers and electric curling irons, mousse or even teasing hair. The beautician used small stiff plastic curling rods, smelly permanent wave solution, tissue wraps, and hard plastic picks that poked into your scalp to hold the rod in place next to your head. The solution soaked into each curl and then you sat for an hour or more with a towel tightly wrapped around your head holding it all in place. After this smelly part was completely done the hairdresser checked for curl. Did the solution work with your hair type? Was the curl tight enough? The idea was to get a tight curl so the permanent would last for months.

If the curl just tested met all the above conditions the rods were carefully loosened and your hair was allowed to be free. Apparently, mine met all the important criteria and the beautician proceeded to remove the curling rods. It felt so good. My hair was short, maybe 3 or 4 inches long. I had worn a ducktail all summer. It was straight in the back, combed forward to my face, short bangs across my forehead.

And now, I was one mass of tight curly frizz! YUK! I screamed. What had she done to me? Who was this starring at me in the mirror? No, it can't be me.

This was an ultra tight curl. A comb couldn't begin to go through this mass of dark brown super thick hair. I could have died.

In a week I was to be on a college campus, outside Chicago. There were going to be students from all over the country. I arrived not even recognizing my own face in the mirror. What had been my mother's good intentions turned into a nightmare.

A young woman did not start college looking like something from outer space. This was 1962.

There was a college look. Name brands weren't in vogue yet, but a look was.

First off, clothes coordinated. Sweater matched skirts, and socks were the same color as your sweater. Panty hose hadn't come on the scene yet. I still had either a garter belt, or a girdle.

Sometimes I still wore nylons with seams and they were seen as a bit dressier. But, I was starting to wear seamless hosiery as more and more young women were seen doing these days. Slacks were only worn for casual events. Pantsuits hadn't made their appearance yet and polyester was just beginning to be worn.

Cotton skirts, requiring ironing, pleated polyester skirts, with matching cardigan sweaters, and wool tweed made up the college "look." A-line and pleated skirts were shown in "Seventeen" and other teen magazines. sweater sets, short pullover sweaters with a matching identical color cardigan and socks, were what fashion magazines were showing.

My parents could not understand my worry about my hair. I knew that it would take all my courage to show up on campus. But to have refused to go. No, that thought never entered my head.

I had planned to go to college for as along as I remembered. I wanted to be somebody, do something, and get away from the country. I could not stay home even for a short time. That to me would admit to failure.

At least, I reasoned to myself, no one knew me there. I would me a new person. Except for my second-cousin Lori I wouldn't know a soul or a soul know me. I guess I figured she and I always liked each other and both being from the country would understand each other. My dad and her grandmother were brother and sister. I would have to trust her to still look at me and maybe even sit with me in the dining hall.

I remember I wore my yellow and white checked shirtwaist sleeveless dress. It showed off my tan. All summer I had taken care of four children in a suburb north of Chicago on Lake Michigan. I had gone to the beach almost every day and I was tanned deeply. This was long before any reports of skin cancer. I had poured baby oil on my skin to help me tan quickly. Even my legs were a deep brown, so that I could get away with not wearing nylons. With flats I wore flesh colored footlets. They were necessary so that my foot didn't get stuck tight in my shoe. And of course, footlets were a lot cooler to wear than nylons.

The president of the college was out in the driveway welcoming the parents as they drove in with their anxious stricken student. This was it. This was to be my home for the next four years.

I had seen the Concordia College campus earlier that summer. My employer, the Mom of the four children, drove over with me one day in July. I didn't know what to expect. To tell the truth I was disappointed. I expected it to be a bigger, more awesome looking campus. In reality, it was a campus of 40 acres nestled in an affluent section of a Western Chicago suburb. It had a pretty front yard. There were big pillars, very academic looking, in the front yard, called the quad. This would be the gathering spot for many sing-a-longs and other campus events.

The classrooms and the hallways looked much like high school. College was supposed to look different, or so I thought in my imagination.

There was a reception for new students and their parents in the College Union. It was there that I first met Becky. My dad could and would talk to anyone. Besides being a teacher full-time, he had many jobs in the summertime: selling insurance, fireman, canning factory, Neenah foundry, painting houses, and haying with the farmers in the summertime. My dad could strike up a conversation with anyone. And so, he started talking with Mr. Baehr from Tonawanda, NY. Tonawanda is near Niagara Falls.

My dad knew Niagara Falls and had a niece who lived there. These two fathers introduced their daughters to each other. It was friendship at first sight.

We were both country girls. We both had very anxious fathers. But nonetheless, there was a down-to-earthiness in common that made us both feel at home with each other and thus at this our new home, away from home we became instant friends. Becky and I started talking, sharing stories and life from that day onward.

To describe Becky, I would have to start with the word bubbly. Becky always had a smile. Her brown eyes sparkled and laughter readily bubbled out of her. She could make any situation humorous and was the first to laugh at herself or the situation she was in. She never seemed to worry and took life one day at a time.

This approach to life would stand her in good stead, as life didn't always treat her with the same good grace as she gave to it.

Becky and I discovered that our assigned dorm rooms were close to each other. We both had the 2nd floor in two different dorms that shared a connecting corridor.

Across from Becky's room were three high school chums from Luther North, a Chicago Lutheran High School. Two of these women, Irma and Ruth would also become friends of mine for life.

As Irma tells the story of how we met, I was down in the laundry room trying to figure out how much money I needed to wash my clothes. The dorm provided indoor clothes lines so students could save money by not using the electric dryer. My parents never even had an automatic washing machine, much less a dryer, so the automatic washer seemed like a real luxury. I didn't have many wash and wear clothes, so the indoor clothesline would suit my clothes and my budget just fine.

Irma remembers my curly hair and how the beanie perched on the top. Oh yes, all freshmen had to wear a beanie, so that we could be easily identified. They were in the school colors: maroon and gold.

Now it couldn't have been too hard to spot freshmen. We were the scared, timid type, trying to find the right building and the right classroom.

If an upper classman saw you, he or she, as the case may be, could ask you to carry their books or worst yet, stop and sing the college school song. The song was a melody I had never heard before. I'm not sure what happened to freshmen who didn't know the song, but I didn't want to find out.

I can still recite the Alma Mater. My singing of it hasn't improved. I think the melody is some minor key, written by a German with no thought of melody.

The words are:

Hail to thee, our alma mater.
Hail to thee, maroon and gold.
Here we stand your sons and daughters
Thinking it back to days of old.
Days of joy and happy meetings.
Days of friendship and of love
Hail to thee, our alma mater,
Hail Concordia, Hail.

After about a month, all freshmen knew the song and we could put our beanies away.

Even though the campus was small, the college managed to place all your classes in different buildings. Most freshmen panicked as five minutes were scheduled between classes. Sometimes there was a break with an open period. But they used the quarter system, so generally most students had five academic classes, plus physical education and music lessons four times a week.

Also, being a Lutheran college and preparing students for the teaching ministry attendance at chapel was mandatory, at least for freshmen. Chapel was held every weekday from 9:45 AM to 10:15 AM. in the gymnasium. The college was planning on building a chapel, but this wouldn't be finished for another ten years after I left the campus.

What is the chemistry that makes friendship binding? How does a person feel at home so quickly with certain people, and others that you know while they are friendly and you exchange helloes, the chemistry isn't there?

Irma and I were friends from the start. Becky, Irma and I, were a trio. Irma's good friend from Luther High, Ruth, also was a freshman and was Irma's roommate along with Virginia, another friend from Luther High.

Ruth was the more serious one. She wore thick glasses, always had a ready smile and was a terrific listener. Ruth had an inquisitive sense of humor. She noticed minute details about people and made you feel special. Ruth was in the choir and had a lovely alto voice, and was an exceptionally good pianist and organist.

Becky also played the piano and organ and really was quite good, but most of all she loved to sing. Irma and I enjoyed music, but were not at the same level as Ruth and Becky. Irma did make a college choir, so I should just speak for myself.

I tried out for the Kapelle Choir, but, was told I would need to practice more with voice lessons. I could have made the general choir, but I couldn't handle that let-down feeling. I figured it was better to just admit defeat. I was going to join the band, but rehearsals interfered with my work schedule, and I really wasn't sure that I was college band material. My cousin Lori also had a lovely voice and was in the Kapelle Choir all through her college years.

It was mandatory for all students to have keyboard lessons. I had to audition to find out my level. The first quarter I was placed with five other students and we went over the rudiments of keyboard theory. I never had paid too much attention to that while having lessons with my mom. The second quarter I had my own piano teacher, Miss Link. By the end of my second year I was considered proficient enough to receive individual organ lessons. I found them always a challenge.

While I enjoyed playing hymns, I never mastered the foot pedal. I have been always grateful for the lessons, as they would stand me in good stead in later years. In several of my future teaching positions I would be the choir director, organist, band director, and often the school's only music teacher.

The quarter of organ lessons I particularly remember though was when I was assigned the instructor who had just graduated from Julliard. He expected his students to practice twelve hours a week. I found this next to impossible to do. In addition to finding the time to practice that long, I wasn't sure I had the talent that would make that much worthwhile.

Lori, my second cousin, was just across the hall from Ruth, Virginia and Irma. Her good friend from home, Janet, was right next door to my room.

Our families had visited back and forth through the years, but not daily as we lived about seventy miles apart. It was always fun going to Lori's house as she lived on a dairy farm in the rolling countryside of the Kettle Moraine.

I remember when we were little Lori seemed so bashful to me. Her parents spoke German at home and she didn't speak English until she started grammar school.

We had lots of fun together. We played games, shared school stories, talked clothes and some baby dolls. For high school, Lori's parents sent her to a Lutheran boarding school, about 40 miles from her home. That sounded so exciting to me. Lori was the oldest in her family with three younger sisters and three younger brothers. The youngest child was born while we were sophomores in college!

Janet, a friend of Lori's from a nearby parish joined our group for many activities. Our fathers were also friends. They both were Lutheran schoolteachers and had been in college together back in the 1920's.

Janet was the true perfectionist. Her dresses, her hair, her fingernails all were perfect. Her schoolwork also was done to exacting standards. She and Ruth were the most studious of our group, with Irma being a close third.

Later on, Puf and Nan would join our little group, and we would make up the robin. Letters between the friends formed this first year at Concordia went back and forth across the country for over thirty years.

Nan was Lori's roommate. She was another Wisconsinite growing up south of Milwaukee. Nan was loving, cheerful, always peppy and on-the-go. She had a steady boy friend Charlie back home, which really impressed us all.

Janet also dated a guy from home, but she also dated on campus. She was small and petite, things I saw as a real advantage. I felt myself tall and gangly.

Irma also dated a few guys from Chicago's Luther High and another real serious ministerial student from the Moody Bible Institute. Ruth dated a talented music student and we all thought they'd get married. We all grieved with Ruth when they broke up.

Lori, Becky and I just talked about guys, dreamed about them and put them all on a pedestal in some mysterious world unknown to us. Another Delores, or Puf, a nickname from her family name, joined our group our junior year. She transferred in from a junior college.

College life was wonderful. There were pillow fights, giggling after the lights went out, talk, talk, and talk, running to class, and getting in lunch lines. Sometimes we walked down to the "L" Chicago's public transit system. It was a fifteen-minute walk. We all would go into the city together. Those of us from the country would gawk at the city slums that we saw as the train rumbled on by. Did people really live like this? It was hard for us to believe.

In our second year of college a few of us signed up to teach Sunday School at an inner city African American parish. We found it ironic and somewhat amusing that the name of the pastor was Rev. White. He was a terrific pastor and had great rapport with his parishioners. As they really needed teachers, most of us were given our own Sunday School class. The minister accepted us as adults and was so appreciative of our willingness to teach the students on a regular basis. It was fun and another learning experience.

I especially remember one Sunday when we were asked to help recruit new members for church and Sunday School. We were to canvas the neighborhood. We were to go out two by two and were given a territory. This was in the era of housing projects. Tall high rises were built as new apartment dwellings to replace the slums. There was little, if any grass. One small paved playground for the hundreds of children who lived in the projects. There were just blocks and blocks of high rises and people packed into a city block.

Becky and I were partners. We decided to split up. We thought we could cover more territory that way. I remember the look of surprise on this one particular African American man as I rang his door bell and started my spiel of inviting him and his family to visit First Immanuel.

He asked, "What are you doing out alone?" I explained how I had a partner, but she was in the next building.

"Don't you know how dangerous that is?" He asked. "You shouldn't be out by yourself."

He went with me to make sure I met my partner. I never forgot his concern because he had made me aware of my 19-year old country girl gullibility.

Looking back on it all, I don't remember having really serious discussions on racism, drugs or any of the issues that are today's headlines. Maybe we were too busy just viewing the world.

We talked over our course work, or a music technique, or maybe somebody's new hair-do, but race riots, poverty, government, that I don't remember. Perhaps we did, but it's all blotted out.

I remember discussions about liturgy, worship and new Biblical interpretations or folk masses, but none of my friends questioned going to church on Sunday. In fact, most of us went to chapel every day at 9:45 AM.

It was a sheltered world. Forty acres surrounded by a rich suburban community. Our longest grasp into the outside world was probably visiting Rosary College, a 15 minute walk away, or cutting across the nearby monastery lawn that was a short cut to the shopping on North Avenue and Jim's Pizza.

1962 was a safe, secure time to be in college.

The one world event that penetrated this secure world was the Bay of Pigs invasion that fall. There was only one television set for the two freshmen girl's dorms. It was down the basement of Lindemann Hall.

Word got out that the President Kennedy was going to give an important speech. I remember thinking how strange it was to watch TV. Since college had begun I barely had time to think of it. I hardly ever took the time to read the newspaper. There he was on TV, our handsome President with that wonderful New England accent. I had actually seen him in person. In fact I had his autograph. I told the story to all my new friends about JFK visiting my hometown high school. In was in May of 1961 before the Wisconsin primary. It was at the invitation of my world history teacher who was president of the Young Democrats of Wisconsin. That day I became a Democrat.

And what was he saying. We might be invaded by Russia. They were deploying missiles in nearby Cuba. We were the most powerful nation on earth, how could that be?

I know we all returned to our rooms terrified and I remember paying closer attention to world events and coming down to watch the evening news when I could. The television news reporters were either Walter Cronkite on CBS or Chet Huntley and David Brinkley on NBC. There were no remote controls to just sit and go click, click, so I switched off between both from one evening to the next. I couldn't decide who I liked better.

The first weeks of college life were over. The Bay of Pigs Invasion was a reminder to us and perhaps the first awakening in us that college life could not be isolated from the real world. Our idealistic world was coming to an end. But not just yet.

Down the long corridor, before the College Bookstore, on the left was the sign on the door that said **DUPLICATING**. Besides my dorm room and college library this was the place I was to spend much of my time while in college.

I was always working to earn my next quarter's tuition. My parents were unable to pay for my tuition. My first year at Concordia I received a scholarship of $500. from the North Wisconsin district church office, but after that I was completely on my own.

I really had wanted to work in the college library. But apparently, so did many other students, and freshmen were low on the totem pole. But Duplicating wasn't a bad place to work. I had a really nice boss, Louise Mischnick. There were also two secretaries Edna and Elva who did much of the typing for the professors. Students did the rest of the work.

It seems such a different time looking back. This was before copiers, computers, and memory typewriters. I think we had correcting IBM typewriters, but not ones with spellchecker.

When a professor needed to have a test typed up, he would often bring it in handwritten. There were also a few women professors at this time; they also relied on the Duplicating Office secretaries to type up their tests. The secretary then had to figure out the handwriting and type it up to make it look like a professional college examination. The next step was to have it proofread. Edna or Elva usually did this with me or another student worker.

Of course the secretary checked to make sure that I didn't have that particular professor for class, or any related class. Then I could proofread it with her. This was a word-by-word process. Some of these tests were ten pages long. Some words we would spell out to each other, others I just glanced over, to make sure the I's were capitalized, the words spelled correctly and so on.

Once the test was proofread, the necessary corrections were made by the typists. Usually these were typed onto a stencil. If the professors' handwriting was extremely bad, the secretary might have done a rough draft on typing paper first. Correcting a stencil was a lot of work.

The special stencil was now given to the student who was in charge of the duplicator machine. This was an offset printing press. Tests were done in black ink. On occasion for special programs, the machine was cleaned and a different color ink was used.

The test then was run-off. Usually it had to dry overnight. The next day the test was collated. We had a wonderful machine called a collator that could take up to twenty different pages and bring them together in the correct order.

I sat down in front of it. There was a foot release. I pressed my foot on the pedal, and pop, a page from each section got pushed forward towards me. I grabbed those, hopefully in correct order and left to right. I then checked for double pages that may have popped out and then stapled them together. I then crisscrossed the tests by tens, so that I could do a quick count on the number of tests. With luck, I had enough copies of each page. As noted, this was before copiers, so I could not easily get another page made. The test was then put in a sealed folder under the professor's name. The order was complete.

I usually worked two to four hours a day in the Duplicating Office. The Duplicating Office usually closed at five. I also worked there several summers, and in the summers I often worked late into the evening. This was the case when special conferences were on campus, and they wanted their newsletter for the next morning.

The campus newsletter always had to be out by the time chapel ended. If I worked the morning shift proofreading Concordia Tidbits always took priority. Any news item a club or professor wanted printed for that day's edition had to be in the Duplicating Office by 8 AM to get included for that day. It was always a rush job, and typos sometimes slipped by, as it was very quickly proofread.

Occasionally if the office wasn't very busy, or the printing press broke down, I had lag time. This was a good time to go behind the cartons of papers and read your book or take a quick nap.

Sometimes I had to run errands for the office, like delivering papers or a program to a professor.

It wasn't until my junior year that the Xerox machine arrived. And what a glorious day it was.

It was a very big machine. My boss, Louise Mischnick had to rearrange the whole office, so that it would fit it in. Special thermal paper was needed. I remember we had fun taking pictures of our hands, and I seem to remember somebody sitting on the new Xerox to take a picture of that part of the anatomy!

At this time, Xerox copies weren't used for tests. Those had to be typed painstakingly by a secretary and proofread. But it did help, when a professor or office needed another document quickly, that did not need to be picture perfect as thermal paper did not give a very clear image or one that lasted. In time thermal images faded.

Sometimes in the office, tickets or other special programs for events were printed. We had an electric cutter, stencil press for posters and also a binding machine for multi-paged documents.

I think the most I earned in Duplicating was $1.09 an hour. That was minimum wage in the early sixties. Working ten to fifteen hours a week paid for most of my college textbooks and the rest I saved for the next semester's room and board and tuition expenses.

The other part of my tuition I earned with babysitting and housework. All through college I had two regular housecleaning jobs, one on Thursday afternoons, and the other on Saturday mornings.

The job on Thursday I earned five dollars to clean a family's house, working from 1:30 to 5. That was my spending money and I would use it for a new purse, writing paper, postage or socks. It didn't leave extra money for snacks, or frivolous things. But I was happy to have the five dollars.

The family's house was only a 20 minute walk from campus. I remember day-dreaming as I cleaned thinking maybe someday I would have a house that nice, and I would clean it for myself.

I didn't mind the vacuuming or dusting, but I really disliked cleaning the bathrooms. I didn't see how anyone could get it so messy week after week. I never met the teenagers; they were in high school. The woman gave me a cookbook at the end of my junior year when she heard I was getting married. After my marriage, I did get to clean my own house.

The house on Saturday was easier to clean than the Thursday house. It was for an elderly lady living in a fancy apartment about a ten-minute walk from campus. The only problem was that she had such old equipment. The sweeper must have been from the 1920's. It didn't have a disposable bag; I had to clean the bag out week after week. But it was easy to get the apartment cleaned on a Saturday morning, and I earned another four dollars and fifty cents. The college recommended that we be paid $1.25 an hour for housekeeping. To earn that much an hour to clean seemed a fair amount of money to me.

My other college jobs were babysitting and selling Avon. I usually had one or two regular babysitting jobs on the weekend. Occasionally I babysat on a school night. I often had evening classes, or there were college activities.

Babysitting was usually fun. I had done lots of it in Wisconsin in my later grade school and high school years, so I had many methods to deal with children. I knew many games and stories. My Mother's Helper job had also well prepared me to deal with all kinds of situations and children.

In the daytime I often took the children for a walk to the park. Babysitting usually involved serving the children dinner, or a bedtime snack and cleaning up the kitchen. But then, when they were in bed, I had the evening to myself, and I could get some homework done and I was earning money while the children slept. The going rate was seventy-five cents an hour.

I don't think I ever made much money selling Avon. It enabled me to get my own cosmetics and try out a bunch of new products. I would buy Avon samples and share them with my housemates. The times I made extra money on an Avon order were a bonanza.

Life was good. I was able to earn enough money working in college and in the summers, that when I graduated from college I was free of debt.

Working did cut into my social life to a certain extent. But I was able to get by on little sleep. I pushed myself to read and write fast. I loved being exposed to all the events happening around campus and Chicago.

My closest friends were more or less on the same financial wavelength. Some needed to work more, others less, but we all respected each other and were happy to be away at school, meeting new friends and having new experiences. Most of us came from families where our mothers had not gone on to college, so we were first generation women in our families at Concordia.

Irma's mother trained as a practical nurse, but I believe all the other mothers were known at this time as housewives. Of the fathers only a few had completed college, so again, we were breaking new ground. Our parents had gone through the depression as young parents. Having their daughters go on to college was a big step. They were proud of us, hoping for us to achieve the dreams of America that was exploding into the fifties along with Sputnik, not sure what the future would hold.

My sophomore year I lived with Irma and her parents. Concordia did not have enough dormitory space for all the students so they made arrangements with local families in the area to board the sophomores.

Irma's dad decided to buy a second car so that Irma could live at home and commute. It was about a thirty minute drive through Chicago traffic. The new car was a Volkswagen bug. But as it was a stick shift, he decided it would be better for us two young women to drive his other car, a Chevy Corvette that had an automatic transmission.

Irma asked me if I would like to live at her home with her and share the commute. I was thrilled. Her parents were so gracious to me, and only charged me minimal room and board. It would allow me to save more money towards tuition.

Irma's parents lived above the church where her dad served as minister to a deaf congregation in Chicago. His study was on the first floor just off the church sanctuary. We visited the service a few times, but usually drove over to the black congregation where we taught Sunday School.

Her dad always signed and spoke the services, so as a child Irma usually attended another church not very far from her parent's house, which also had a Lutheran school.

Irma's parents always watched the news with Chet Huntley and David Brinkley. When we could, we would have dinner with them. After the meal, we would clean up the kitchen and do our homework.

Irma's mother would then go to bed for a few hours, as she had the night shift as the evening nurse. As she didn't drive a car, she had to catch two buses to get to the hospital. Pastor Scheibert sometimes drove her, but he often had other church duties. She would get home just as we were getting ready for classes in the morning.

I was so grateful to the Scheibert's and how willingly they opened their home to me. Irma's dad was warm and loving with always a twinkle in his eye.

Irma's mom was a dear, but I felt bad as she often was very tired from working the night shift and keeping up all the duties expected from her as a minister's wife. Pastor Scheibert helped out in the kitchen and with cleaning, which was a new experience for me to witness.

It was a very special year, and before long I would be dating a student who was a shuttle bus driver for those students not having a car of their own.

Earlier, I told about the day of John F. Kennedy's assassination. I was a sophomore that year. It tore into my sheltered world and made me take another look at America. It made history seem even more real, and helped me realize that I was connected to a wider world than just Concordia or Wisconsin. My mother's saying, "Someday birdie you too may fly away," was becoming reality. I was learning of a wider world and was being drawn into seeing this world for myself. I still had a lot to learn, but I was getting ready to fly off on my own.

POTATO DONUTS

1 1/4 cup sugar
2 Tablespoons of shortening
Mix with sugar.
2 eggs
1 cup milk
1 cup mashed potato
Beat all together.

Dry ingredients:
- 5 cups flour
- 3 teaspoons baking powder
- 1 teaspoon salt
- 1 teaspoon nutmeg
- 1 teaspoon ginger

Sift little by little into liquid and beat.
After all the flour is in the liquid
Place dough onto floured board.
Flour your board with about 1/2 cup flour.
Dough will be sticky.
Work in little of flour
Roll dough about 1/2 inch thick.
Cut doughnuts out with doughnut cutter or a round cookie cutter.
Deep fry in lard or vegetable oil heated in electric frying pan, set at 375 degrees.
Turn only once.
Set on paper towels to cool.
Roll in sugar and enjoy.

Store a few away in a plastic container to enjoy another day.

EPILOGUE

Childhood, what a mixture of emotions? Much to my surprise as I looked back on my youth, I realized the happy moments far outweighed the sad. I'd like to share this Bible verse that has had so much meaning for me….

"Let your heart give you joy in the days of your youth."
Ecclesiastes 11 verse 9

Thank you for taking the journey with me.

Books by Pearn and Associates, Inc.

The Great Adventure—Untold, Charles Hamman, nonfiction, cloth*
Cowboy Up, Ryan Thorburn, nonfiction, paper
1945, Joseph J. Kozma, novel, paper*
Light Across the Alley, *The Story of a Young Matchmaker,* Victor W. Pearn (Fiction) Kindle Books only*
Dream Season, *My Brother Gary and the 1957 Ashland Panthers* Victor W. Pearn (Biography) Kindle Books only*
Until We Meet, Joseph J. Kozma (Poetry) paperback
It Started & Ended: **The Story About a Soldier and Civilian Life**, Bud Grounds (Biography) paper
Lost Cowboys: The Bud Daniel Story, and Wyoming Baseball, Ryan Thorburn (Biography) paper
Black 14: The Rise, Fall and Rebirth of Wyoming Football, Ryan Thorburn (Biography) paper
The Dreamer and the Dream, Rick E. Roberts (Poetry) paper
Mathematics in Color, Joseph J. Kozma (Poetry) paper
Walking in Snow, John Knoepfle (Poetry) paper
I Look Around for my Life, John Knoepfle (Biography) cloth and Kindle*
A Lenten Journey Toward Christian Maturity, William E. Breslin (Prayer Guide) paper
Ikaria: A Love Odyssey on a Greek Island, Anita Sullivan (Biography) paper and Kindle*
The U Book, Photo Travel Journal in India, Nathan Pierce (Poetry & Biography — publisher only) full color paper
Another Chance, Joe Naiman, (Fiction — publisher only) cloth
Goulash and Picking Pickles, Louise Hoffmann (Biography) cloth
Point Guard, Victor Pearn (Fiction) cloth

Available on Barnesandnoble.com, Amazon.com, (also available from Ingram Books and Baker and Taylor) you may order from your local bookstore, or from the publisher — Pearn and Associates, Inc. happypoet@hotmail.com/970-599-8924.
*Available on Kindle Books.

www.ingramcontent.com/pod-product-compliance
Lightning Source LLC
LaVergne TN
LVHW091034080826
845145LV00002B/496

* 9 7 8 0 9 8 4 6 5 2 3 5 8 *